3. 95

THE FLESH: INSTRUMENT OF SALVATION
Caro Salutis est Cardo

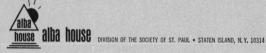

alba house DIVISION OF THE SOCIETY OF ST. PAUL • STATEN ISLAND, N.Y. 10314

THE FLESH
INSTRUMENT
OF SALVATION

A THEOLOGY
OF THE HUMAN
BODY

CIPRIANO
VAGAGGINI
O.S.B.

Translated by Rev. Charles Underhill Quinn
Original title: Caro Salutis Est Cardo — Corporetà, Eucaristia e Liturgia
Published by Desclée & Co., Rome, Italy

Nihil Obstat:
Gall Higgins, O.F.M., Cap.

Imprimatur:
Joseph P. O'Brien, S.T.D. — Vicar General
New York, N.Y. — October 29, 1968

Library of Congress Catalog Card Number: 69-15856

Designed, printed and bound in the U.S.A. by the Pauline Fathers and Brothers of the Society of St. Paul at Staten Island, New York as a part of their communications apostolate.

"Do you not know that your bodies are members of Christ?"
(I Cor. 6:15)

"Those who are well have no need for a physician, but those who are sick: I came not to call the righteous, but sinners."
(Mk. 2:17).

FOREWORD

As odd as it might seem at first, anthropology — how we understand man in general — has a determining influence on the other branches of what may be called the moral sciences, including theology. How we approach theology depends to a large extent upon a particular view of man. This is also true in the area of theoretical or practical spirituality and in pastoral theology. The reason is that man is a complex being, a body and a soul. His spiritual faculties are the intellect and the will, and the intellect has a conceptual and reasoning function, an experimental intuitive function, etc.

The manner of looking at complex beings varies. Without denying any one of the component elements, we may still emphasize one over another or value one more than the other within the over-all composite. There are very many practical consequences resulting from the way in which we understand and compose our theology, and the way that we understand and practice the spiritual and pastoral life, depending on whether we give first place in man's faculties to the will or affectivity in general rather than to the intellect, or whether we give first place among the intellect's functions to intuition instead of to the abstract concept and the power of reasoning. This is all the more true if we place no trust in the conceptual and reasoning function, or if we underrate it. But it does not necessarily follow that we have to fall into the subjectivism or relativism of some of our contemporaries if we agree with them in saying that all problems, and most especially religious ones, have an anthropological focus pertaining to the meaning of man and life itself. Is this special focus not the greatest stimulus towards a fuller examination of these problems and even a decisive factor in our formulation and resolution of them?

What is true for these moral sciences is also true in the case of the liturgy. Our aim in this study is to show how important it is for us to have a proper evaluation of the function of man's body in understanding the liturgy, particularly for an understanding of it in three central points: the place held in the liturgy by the paschal mystery, the centrality of the eucharistic mystery, and finally the position occupied by the liturgy in the whole life of the Church where it is the apex at which everything converges and the source from which everything flows.

TABLE OF CONTENTS

I

THE PROBLEM

1) Corporeity and the Catholic faith in general

Catholic faith in general strongly insists upon the substantial union between body and soul, spirituality and the soul's transcendence notwithstanding. For this reason man is not the soul. Nor is the soul disincarnate, or merely enclosed within the body as in a jacket, a prison or a tomb. To the Catholic, man is the substantial complex of body and soul. For this reason the composite of these two elements is so intimate that each of the two components is conceived as a complement of the other by its intrinsic nature, and together they form a unique entity that is independent and stands by itself. Hence the component parts are not of themselves complete and independent self-standing entities but only parts of a complete and independent being.

Our intention here is not to give any long documentation showing that this really is the thought of the magisterium on this point,[1] nor to examine the problems arising from this assertion when compared with the affirmation of the soul's spirituality and its survival even without the body. For our purposes it is enough that faith affirms the substantial union of body and soul as well as the soul's spirituality and transcendence.

2) Unconscious dualism

On the contrary, we have to stress another fact. Without being aware of it, and inspite of the theoretical faith we profess, we are often dualistic. We think and at times even act as if man were essentially only soul.

Here are a few examples from common speech, which are all the more meaningful since we use them spontaneously and unwittingly. We say generally that what is important when all is said and done is that we save our soul. We speak of undertaking a mission or preparing ourselves for the ministry so that we might save souls. We say: *salus animarum suprema lex; da mihi animas cetera tolle.* When we want to say how many persons, how many parishioners are in our parish, we say we have a certain number of souls. Of a saintly man we say that he is a holy soul, a beautiful soul, a soul dear to God. Of a person suffering we say that he is a soul in pain, a troubled soul.

The struggle St. Paul speaks of between the "flesh" and the "spirit" we interpret simplistically as a struggle between the soul and the body. In a similar context we easily adopt St. Francis' expression, calling the body "brother jackass."[2]

---

1. For example at the Council of Vienne in 1312 against certain theories of Pietro Olivi. See **Denzinger-Schönmetzer** 902 (481) together with 1440 (738). Pius IX confirmed the same notions in 1867 against the theories of Anton Günther (**ibid.** 2828 [1655]) and Leo XIII in 1893 in his review of certain propositions of Rosmini (**ibid.** [1941]).

2. Epictetus, **Convers,** (rep. in **Anianus** 4, 1); **Dissert.** IV 1, 17.

It is still not too uncommon in translations of the Gospels to have Jesus' words, recorded in Matthew 16:26 and Mark 8:36, rendered in this fashion: "What will it profit a man if he gains the whole world and loses his soul?" Here we see put in relief the need to save one's soul at the price of losing all the rest, including the body, although from the context and the sense that the Greek work *psyche* has there, Jesus is not speaking of saving the "soul" at the price of losing the body, but of saving life, the true everlasting life of the soul and the body, at the cost, if necessary, of the sacrifice of our present life.

Obviously in these and similar expressions we are fully aware of what they really mean. We in no way wish to deny the belief in the substantial unity of body and soul. Seen in the light of the intention of those using them, these expressions are aimed merely at affirming the superiority of one of the two elements of the substantial human composite over the other, i.e. the soul over the body. There is no doubt about this. But this does not take away from the fact that as they stand, these expressions are technically imprecise, and that their own lack of precision comes from and is nurtured by a subconscious notion which, if we thought about it and accepted it, would imply dualism.

How did this happen? Our answer will be lengthy and we shall have to investigate both the ancient and more recent influences. Through different paths and with different shades of meaning — often contrary to the people's practical way of acting, particularly in the case of Greece, where they went against the general humanistic tendency of ordinary Greek culture — all the ancient philosophies arrived at a certain dualism where the body was looked upon as the natural enemy of the soul, its clothing, its burden, its prison, its tomb (*soma-sema*), into which the soul had fallen as a result of some metaphysical, cosmological or moral pre-earthly incident. With the body, the soul had to act and live with prudence, but it also had to find a way to be as completely free of it as possible and, as soon as it could, to rejoin its own *summum bonum*.[3]

Therefore, especially in the Orphic, Pythagorean, Platonist[4] and neo-Platonist traditions — and in its way also the Stoic tradition — we find considerable influence that was also to affect Christian thinkers.

In addition, with some ancient and medieval thinkers, we find the temptation to dualism of a Gnostic, Encratistic or Manichean type.[5]

We see this especially, whether in antiquity or during the Renaissance and modern times, coming as a reaction against paganizing hedonism, (of a humanistic type in antiquity and during the Renaissance, and materialistic in modern times).

Finally, we have the influence of Protestantism and then of the humano-moral ideal of the Idealists and Illuminists, with their notion of religion as a purely internal and personal thing, and with their scorn for what they called popular and ritual religion.

Apart from particular heresies, these trends and influences did not infect the specifically Christian balance of orthodox writers in the reflex question of the relations between soul and body. But with some of their number and in our own common parlance there are traces of a particular dualistic-spiritualistic mentality that has not been completely reabsorbed.

3) *Consequent misunderstandings about the liturgy*

This more or less conscious dualism is one of the major obstacles to the understanding of the true nature of the liturgy and its function in the life of the Church.

---

3. See the outline in D. Gorce, **Corps**, in: **Dictionnaire de spiritualité**, II (1953) 2338-42.

4. Plato's characteristic expression: "The soul of the philosopher completely scorns the body and flees it as it seeks to become isolated within itself." **Phaedo** 65c.

5. See the brief outline in Gorce's article 2345-51.

In order to understand today in a generic way this con-
catenation of problems we must take note of the following
facts. The recent documents of the magisterium never tire of
repeating that central to the liturgy is the celebration of the
Eucharist,[6] that indeed the whole liturgy in a special way, in
its center, which is the eucharistic mystery, has no other object
than to draw men by the means willed by God into the paschal
mystery. Living this mystery summarizes and expresses the
whole of the Christian economy.[7]

It is within this eucharistic and paschal context that the
second Vatican Council proclaimed the doctrine of the liturgy
as the summit and source of both the spiritual and pastoral
life of the Church.[8]

As a matter of fact, unless we have a clear perception of
the centrality held by the paschal mystery within the economy
of salvation willed by God and the irreplaceable function
which the eucharistic mystery has in making this a reality in
every man, we cannot comprehend the true nature of the
liturgy. And especially, we shall be incapable of understanding
how it can be the summit and the source of the Church's life.

The true understanding of the centrality of the paschal
mystery and the Eucharist's irreplaceable function in making
this a reality in men is far from being generally grasped. This
we can see from the discussions revolving around the Constitution on the Liturgy of Vatican II. So many objections,
particularly against the doctrine of the liturgy as the summit
and source of the life of the Church, originated from this lack
of understanding.

---

6. Vatican II, **Const. on the Lit.**, art. 6; 7; 10; 41; 47-49; **Const. on
the Church**, art. 11; sacrificium eucharisticum totius vitae christianae
fontem et culmen; art. 26: in eucharistia continuo vivit et crescit Ecclesia;
art. 28, **Decree on Ecumenism**, art. 2; 15; 22.

7. Vatican II, **Const. on the lit.**, art. 5; 6; 47; 61; 81., and most explicitly in the **Instruction** of Sept. 26th, 1964, no. 6. See also Vatican II,
Decree on Ecum., art. 2; 22.

8. Vatican II, **Const. on the lit.**, art. 9.

Where is the root of this defect? In my opinion it is to be found in a contemporary anthropology that is unwittingly faulty. Without our realizing it, there is a survival in us of a kind of dualism resulting from an exaggeratedly spiritualistic idea of man. The body and its function in human nature are scorned in favor of the soul.

We therefore no longer understand how within the means of salvation willed by God the physical body of Christ possesses a function *that is always active and permanent and even eternal.* Consequently we no longer clearly see the function of the resurrection of Christ — and therefore that of the paschal mystery and of our own resurrection — nor the function of the eucharistic mystery. Actually, we can understand both of these notions and therefore the true nature of the liturgy only when we realize the ever active and permanent part willed by God that is played by the physical body of Christ in the accomplishment of salvation in us.

I feel that it is most urgent that all of us be reminded of this reality and become aware of it.

II

MAN'S CORPOREITY IN THE BIBLE

An unwittingly dualistic mentality is not adapted for understanding the spirit of genuine Christian tradition in examining the relations between soul and body. In the first place it is not capable of understanding Scripture in this area.

1) *The Greek and biblical ways of looking upon man*

At this juncture we are greatly helped by the fact that recent studies have given us a global, intuitive, concrete and — if I may say so — existential way of looking at, thinking about and representing Semitic and particularly biblical tradition, in contradistinction, for example, to the analytical, abstract and therefore essentialistic and metaphysical views of Greek philosophy.[1]

---

1. See J. Pedersen, **Israel, Its Life and Culture** (London, 1926), H. W. Robinson, "Hebrew Psychology" in **The People and the Book**, ed.

This is of enormous importance for the interpretation of the Bible and for the way we use it in theology. But to acknowledge the general correctness of this observation and its decisive bearing on the whole of theology does not mean that we must necessarily fall into the antimetaphysical and antispeculative excesses of a Bultmann or of some who follow too closely upon his footsteps. They stress so much that the outlook of Scripture and its modes of expression are global, intuitive and concrete, that they appear to deny or at least underrate the fact that there are statements in the Bible that have a properly ontological and metaphysical value that is at the least implicit and can legitimately be brought to light.

Nevertheless, the following observations will help us see how important the biblical manner of looking at things in a global, intuitive and concrete way is for an understanding of man himself.

When the Greek notion is exaggerated to the point of error, man is conceived essentially as a soul enclosed within a body through some cosmological or moral incident. When this mode of thought is not erroneous, man is considered to be an embodied soul.

This view of man is the result of an analytical reflexion which in a particular man, John Doe, is concerned primarily with his various parts or of the various aspects that go to make him up. It is concerned with specifying a particular nature through distinguishing essence from accidents, with evaluating and ordering hierarchically the single parts that have been analyzed in the reciprocal relationship they share with one another. The result of this analysis is that the soul is found to be on the first plane of our attention. The difference of its

---

by A. S. Peake (Oxford, 1925) pp. 352-382. Claude Tresmontant, **Essai sur la pensée hébraïque**, Lectio divina 12, (Paris, 1952), and by the same author, **Etudes de métaphysique biblique** (Paris, 1955). Thorleif Boman, **Das hebräische Denken im Vergleich mit dem griechischen**, Göttingen, 1959).

nature from that of the body and its transcendence in relationship to the body are strongly accentuated.

In the biblical perspective, however, man is an *animate* body with a soul that has a much more divine origin than the body.

We may therefore reach the conclusion that between the correct Greek mode of thinking and the scriptural notion there is merely a shade of difference. That is true, but this nuance is most important.

The Bible looks at man primarily as he appears concretely and globally to the senses, the imagination, and in its way, the intelligence: substance and accidents as found in a particular John Doe.

Therefore corporeity — not a static corporeity but one that is dynamic, a body that *moves* — is on the first level of perception, attention and expression. The soul and its more divine origin is a trait, so to speak, that is joined to it in a second psychological moment: man is a body that moves, which is quite distinct from other moving bodies. He is a body animated by a soul that has a very special origin. It is this notion that underlies the account of man's creation in Genesis 2:7.

In the Greek philosophical context, corporeity, the substantial union of body and soul, remains difficult to explain. Without yet touching on the Eucharist, the dogmas of the incarnation and the resurrection, in the light of this, yoke together ideas which at the very least are paradoxical.

However in the context of the Hebrew Bible, corporeity presents no difficulty. It is the pure spirituality of the soul and its immortality that remain obscure. In fact, we may say that Scripture is not at all concerned with such precise philosophical questions about the soul.

It is well known that spirituality as a natural endowment of the soul is only implied in the Bible. As for the idea of the soul's survival without the body, it is clearly found only toward the end of Old Testament times, and Scripture does not take up the question of whether such a survival is natural to the soul or a special gift of God. However, the idea of the survival of the whole man, body and soul, is quite an old one in biblical tradition (the concept of *She'ol*).

The fact stands that in its perspective of man the Bible does not separate the body from the soul. According to Scripture, in the religious history of man, the body is looked upon above all as a "coprotagonist" along with the soul, both the subject and the object of action. It will be enough for us to recall summarily the chief points.

2) *Creation and fall*

In the imaginative account of the creation of man in Genesis, God with greatest care forms the body and then the soul with his breath (Genesis 2:7-22). The whole concrete man, body and soul, was made in God's image insofar as the whole man is called to exercise his dominion over all creation as a stewardship (Genesis 1:26-28). Those things which later theology has called the preternatural gifts granted by God to man before the fall in order to make him a perfect being in his own natural line, refer in Scripture to the whole man. Immortality (*aphtharsia*), impassibility, and immunity from concupiscence are especially directed toward the body. But the dominion exercised over created things that we have just mentioned also includes the body. Nor is it excluded from the gift of *gnosis* (knowledge) since, as the Fathers rightly remind us, this is not a question of a purely profane conceptual and abstract knowledge but of a religious knowledge that is more intuitive and affective — an inclination to contemplation in which the whole concrete being is fully involved.

Moreover, in its description of man before sin, Scripture does not analyze the various aspects and levels in which man exists. It does not make any distinction among natural endowments, grace and preternatural gifts. It describes the first men concretely in a state of perfect happiness, both bodily and otherwise, in perfect harmony with God, and — as Genesis 3:24 supposes — with the angels and of course with lesser creation. The distinction between these various levels we have mentioned is both legitimate and necessary, and can deduced from the totality of biblical data. However, a further reflection and analysis is required with which the Bible, in its emphasis on a concrete consideration of man, does not concern itself.

The fall is the fall of concrete man, both body and soul, and "death" which is its punishment in the Bible is both a physical and a spiritual death, one implying the other. The reason for this is that for the Bible physical death is a consequence of sin and the overcoming of sin in last analysis always also includes the overcoming of physical death in the resurrection of the body.[2]

3) Body and redemption in general

In the creation and the fall as well as in the redemption, the body is no less subject and object than the soul. What is lost, must be saved, and is saved, is not the soul but the whole man.

Furthermore redemption in the Bible is looked upon as a return to the original paradise, but in a more sublime form. There all was perfect: concrete man, body and soul, his relations with God and the angels, that sub-human world which was the theater in which man lived in compliance with his state of perfection and complete happiness. According to Scripture, in a more sublime way, this will be the lot of saved man.

For St. Paul the body is eminently the object of redemption. In this light he told us: "you will be temples of the Holy Spirit"

---

2. See 1 Corinthians 15:26; Revelation 20:14. Also, "Le mystère de la mort" in **Lex orandi 12** (Paris, 1954). R. Bultmann, in **Theolog. Wörterbuch zum NT**, III (1938), 15-21.

(1 Corinthians 3:16), "you are the body of Christ and his members" (1 Corinthians 12:27), "you belong to Christ" (1 Corinthians 3:23; 6:19). And he also said: "your body is the temple of the Holy Spirit" (1 Corinthians 6:19-20), "your body is a member of Christ" (1 Corinthians 6:16), "your body belongs to Christ" (1 Corinthians 6:13). This is preceded by that most vivid expression: "the body is not meant for immorality, but for the Lord, and *the Lord for the body*." Does this not imply an almost disconcerting concreteness for us?

4) *Body and resurrection*

Let us admit that in this context, in the unconscious mentality of disincarnate spiritualism shared by many of us, St. Paul's extraordinary insistence upon our future resurrection sounds strange. On this point he had continually to fight against the spirit of the Greeks (Acts 17:32; 1 Corinthians 15; 2 Timothy 2:18).

Those Corinthians whom he admonished in 1 Corinthians 15 did not deny the resurrection of Christ. They most probably admitted it as an extraordinary privilege. They therefore did not deny, absolutely speaking, that God was able to raise the dead. But they did deny our resurrection. Why? What were their motives? St. Paul does not tell us. But we are obviously referred to the exaggerated spiritualism of the Greeks which saw man's whole perfection and beatitude in the soul and was unable to see the usefulness of the body in this area.

At Corinth there already existed that theory, later broadcast by Hymenaeus and Philetus, and mentioned in 2 Timothy 2:18. They said that "the resurrection is past already," and therefore limited it to the regeneration of the soul through faith and baptism.

For us St. Paul's response to the Corinthians is disconcerting when he says that they did not deny the possibility that God can raise the dead but only the fact that he raises us.

Actually St. Paul said: "For if the dead are not raised, then Christ has not been raised. If Christ has not been raised, your faith is futile and you are still in your sins. Then those who also have fallen asleep in Christ have perished. If for this life only we have hoped in Christ, we are of all men most to be pitied. . . . If the dead are not raised, 'Let us eat and drink, for tomorrow we die.'. . . When the perishable puts on the imperishable, and the mortal puts on immortality, then shall come to pass the saying that is written: 'Death is swallowed up in victory. O death, where is thy victory? O death where is thy sting?' The sting of death is sin, and the power of sin is the law. But thanks be to God, who gives us the victory through our Lord Jesus Christ" (1 Corinthians 15:16-19; 32:53-57).

In this text St. Paul's wish is to reduce the Corinthians' position to the absurd by reasoning in this way: if we shall not rise then 1.) Christ is not risen. For St. Paul there is a necessary connection between our resurrection and Christ's: if we shall not rise then Christ is not risen; if Christ is risen then we too shall rise; 2.) if we shall not rise our faith is vain and we are still in our sins; our sufferings are vain and we are the most wretched of men; 3.) this is absurd, and 4.) it is therefore necessary that we rise.

In the explanation given by the commentators to these passages, there is much that is obscure. On the one hand they realize that the Corinthians were not denying the possibility that God can raise the dead, but on the other hand in this hypothesis St. Paul's argumentation does not seem to persuade.

The difficulty of the first conclusion (if we shall not rise then Christ is not risen) has been raised by St. Thomas who observes: "it seems that this argumentation is not valid . . . if Christ has risen by a special divine power it does not follow that other men will rise."[3] Nor would it seem that if other men rise, Christ also must have risen.

---

3. In 1 Cor., 15:16.

St. John Chrysostom formulates the difficulty in St. Paul's second conclusion in this way: "What are you saying, Paul? How can we hope only in this life if the bodies do not rise, when there remains the soul which is immortal?"[4]

Two difficulties of a specifically Greek variety. The first one comes from not putting oneself in Paul's context. Between Christ's resurrection and ours he does not wish to establish a connection of metaphysical necessity as if God could not act otherwise, but an historical connection willed by God. He is not inculcating a principle of metaphysics, but the statement of faith that God placed a necessary connection between Christ's resurrection and our own; he willed that Christ rise in order to raise us also and that we should not be raised except through the risen Christ.

Therefore, on the historical plane, Christ's resurrection does not exist without ours, nor does ours without Christ's. In the context of God's plan, Christ is incomprehensible without Christians, just as are Christians without Christ.

The second difficulty is also a typical expression of the Greek mentality and its way of looking at man, a thing which St. Paul is combatting. St. Paul, as the Bible as a whole, does not conceive of man without his body, nor does he look upon man's perfection and total happiness — which is a total submission to God and to his will in our regard — without the perfection of his body: namely, without its being totally penetrated by the divine life, or "spiritualized."

If we observe that St. Paul's phrase (that if we hope in Christ only in this world we are the most miserable of men) is not true, since we have the joy of a right conscience, etc., we are again restricting man's essence to the soul alone and solely to its interiority in a perspective that is totally foreign to Scripture. This would mean that we should be determining the

---

4. In 1 Cor. Hom. 39, 3 PG 61, 335.

perfection and happiness of men by arbitrarily putting aside what is God's will for them.

St. Paul, then, is able to conclude that it is necessary that our mortal being put on immortality. This "necessity" is not to be understood as merely "fitting" in this instance. "Befitting" would be a proper word for the resurrection of the body in relation to the natural and metaphysical order, but it is not strong enough when we are speaking of the concrete order willed by God. Here the word "necessary" is obligatory.

Elsewhere (Romans 8:11-25) St. Paul states that as long as we do not have the "redemption of our bodies," the glorious resurrection, we do not yet have "the adoption as sons," but we still "groan inwardly as we wait" (Romans 8:23). A few verses before this point, however, (vv. 15-16) he had said that all of us who are baptized have received the Spirit of adoption as sons and that the Spirit bears witness in us that we are sons of God. For him, therefore, this means that sonship and redemption essentially include the glorious resurrection of the body.

5) *Body and cosmic unity*

More than that, for St. Paul the glorious resurrection of the bodies of the righteous is such an essential part of redemption that not only do we groan inwardly as we await it, but the whole anxious expectation of the created world is directed toward it as it is oriented toward the "revelation of the sons of God."

The lesser creature awaits it as the liberation from its own slavery of corruption (to which futility it was subjected not by its own initiative but to obey God) and as a participation in the glorious freedom that the sons of God will then obtain. In this expectation "the whole creation has been groaning in travail together until now" (Romans 8:19-22).

In man's lot, the resurrection of the body has an importance that is cosmic and not marginal or secondary. Only then shall inferior creation be liberated!

And this is another most relevant characteristic. Only within the perspective of the co-essential function of the body in man and his history, a function which in God's plan calls for the resurrection of the body, can we understand the intimate unity that unites the various levels of the cosmos in this same plan. Only in this way can we see the cosmic dimension the creation of man has in the Bible,[5] together with man's elevation, fall, redemption and his attainment of the final destiny assigned to him by God. All of this is also of real concern to lesser creation because its relationship to man within God's historical plan depends every time on man's own relationship with God. Indeed, it was created to aid concrete man, who only in his corporeity comes to an immediate contact with the world, to reach those goals of life that God has prescribed for him.

6) *Body and Christian asceticism*

Insofar as the whole man is inclined toward sin and can easily become its slave, Christian life necessarily includes a panoply of bodily mortifications,[6] and is careful not to limit

---

5. See Genesis 1 and 2; Isaiah 11:6-9; 29:17; 30:23-26; 32:13-21; 35:1-10; 65:17-25; 66:22; Joel 3:16-21; Romans 8:19-22; 2 Peter 3:13; Revelation 5:8-14; 21:1-5. In the texts of Genesis 1 and 2, Romans 8:19-22, and in the texts from Revelation, it seems to me that we are dealing not merely with metaphorical expressions that are only intended to in-- dicate the change in customs and sentiments of one society, but with a real connection in God's plan between the cosmos and man in the various phases of his history. See also L. López, "El mundo solidario del hombre en el AT" in **Studium 5** (1965), 217-271.

6. 1 Corinthians 6:12-20; 9:27: "I pommel my body and subdue it, lest after preaching to others I myself should be disqualified." Romans 6:19-23; The worship in spirit owed by the Christian to God is to offer our bodies as a live and holy victim acceptable to God. See also Matthew 10:28.

mortification solely to the interiority of the soul or to the affective sphere alone.[7] But it also strongly shuns any motivation that would have a dualistic tinge.[8] The body is mortified not because it is wicked in itself or because it is the prison of or a drawback to the soul — something from which the soul has to strive to free itself — but simply because the whole concrete man, since he is susceptible or prone to sin, must mortify himself. And "concrete man" means *both* body and soul.

The goal of this mortification, as well as the desire to die that the Christian may eventually have, is the welfare of the body itself — to attain to the final glorious resurrection — as well as that of the soul, since, once again, the purpose of these mortifications is the good of the whole man.[9]

The desire to die, to give up our earthly abode, our "tent," that keeps us far from the Lord, is not the desire to be freed

---

7. Colossians 1, 24: "Now I rejoice in my sufferings for your sake, and in my flesh I complete what is lacking in Christ's afflictions for the sake of his body, that is, the Church"; Philippians 1:20: "With full courage now as always Christ will be honored in my body, whether by life or by death."

8. Colossians 2:20-23.

9. Philippians 1:21, 23; Galatians 2:18. 2 Corinthians 4:16-5:10 is characteristic: "Though our outer nature is wasting away, our inner nature is being renewed every day. For this slight momentary affliction is preparing for us an eternal weight of glory beyond all comparison. . . . For we know that if the earthly tent we live in is destroyed, we have a building from God, a house not made with hands, eternal in the heavens. Here indeed we groan, and long to put on our heavenly dwelling, so that by putting it on we may not be found naked. For while we are still in this tent, we sigh with anxiety; not that we would be unclothed, but that we would be further clothed, so that what is mortal may be swallowed up by life. He who has prepared us for this very thing is God, who has given us the Spirit as a guarantee. So we are always of good courage; we know that while we are at home in the body we are away from the Lord . . . we would rather be away from the body and at home with the Lord. . . . For we must all appear before the judgment seat of Christ, so that each one may receive good or evil, according to what he has done in the body."

from the body, but *from the corruptible state* in which it now
finds itself, and to put on its state of incorruption, a state that
is "spiritual" in that it is compenetrated with the divine life in
the Spirit. In the state of incorruptibility and glory, the body
will no longer be a veil between us and the Lord. Then we shall
always be with him and we shall see him.

Therefore, even the expression "outward man — inner man,"
which is of Greek origin and in Greek tradition is tinged with
dualism, for St. Paul does not mean "body — soul."

On the contrary, it means the whole concrete man, body
and soul, with all that the present life involves for him. It includes on the one hand elements that are temporary, fragile
and even sinful (outward man), and on the other hand definitive elements and endowments that will be preserved in the
future life because they are not subject to corruptibility (inner
man).

In this light, it is clear that the struggle between *sarx* and
pneuma about which St. Paul speaks elsewhere (Romans 6:6-8;
25) does not coincide with the struggle between body and
soul as found in Greek and Hellenistic tradition. On the contrary, it points up the opposition between the tendency toward
sin existing in concrete man, body and soul (which is called
sarx, palaios anthropos, or *soma tes hamartias, soma tou
thanatou*), and the principle of divine life and of the tendency
toward God which, especially after baptism, pervades the
whole man, body and soul, and is called *new man, pneuma,
pneumatic man.*

In summation, the purpose of the Christian life, both in the
sacramental life (Romans 6:3-6) and in the exercise of asceticism, is to participate both in body and soul in the death of
Christ in order to arrive at the resurrection both of the body
and the soul with him, and to attain to a likeness of him. To
know Christ, to win Christ, to be found in Christ, to be together with him, to grasp and as it were to seize Christ, are all
concepts with which St. Paul sums up in one word the life of
a Christian (Philippians 3:8-14). And for the Apostle these

expressions include winning him, and being in and with him, *with our glorious body*. The Christian life is "to know Christ and the power of his resurrection, to share his sufferings, becoming like him in his death, in order to attain the resurrection from the dead" (Philippians 3:10-11).

2 The Flesh

III

CHRISTOLOGY AND CORPOREITY IN THE NEW TESTAMENT

This brief outline we have given of the doctrine of man's corporeity in the Bible takes on its full meaning if we complete it with a sketch of what the Bible has to tell us about corporeity in Christ himself and its function in the work of our salvation according to the historical plan willed by God.

1) *The incarnation*

Greek culture was somewhat prepared to admit the appearance of a God on earth in human form, at least extrinsically, and even the divinization or better, the heroicization, of a man. But it was not ready to admit that God, properly speaking (with the exception of the divine transcendence), could become man. And it was even less willing to admit that he would have assumed a body that would be God's body in the sense (although in a different manner) that in us the body together with the soul not only belongs to man but actually *is* man.

However, a consequence of the biblical view of man and the human body had to be to assign, proportionately of course, to the physical body in Christ and in his work of saving the world that same function that it assigned in general to the body in man and in his activity. This brings us to the New Testament.

Pauline texts, like Romans 8:3 and Philippians 2:6-7, which state that the Son of God appeared *like* us, do not imply any Docetism nor less any Greek type dualism. They teach, rather, that although Christ was a true man like us, he was not like us a sinner, and always remained God even though he was a man.

The importance he gave to the body of Christ in his person and in his work of the salvation of the world was underlined excellently by St. Paul in Colossians 2:9: "In him the whole fullness of deity dwells bodily." What did he mean by this?

He meant that the totality of the divine power which fills the world and which practically speaking is nothing else than the divinity considered dynamically as it works in the world, is present permanently in Christ. It is present *somatikos,* i.e. not *asomatos,* as in the Word before the incarnation, but in the physical body of Christ which is now a glorious body, the body of his glory (Philippians 3:21).

For Paul, as for the whole of Scripture, man is an animate body. He can therefore express the notion that Christ is the Son of God incarnate by saying that the fullness of divinity dwells *bodily* in Christ, or in his body. We find ourselves here with an expression that is the equivalent of St. John's *Verbum caro factum est.*

Only in the Epistle to the Colossians does Paul use so characteristic an expression. We might wonder at the reason for this. I believe that there is serious reason here to maintain that he was inspired to do so as a polemic against the false teachers of Colossae whom he has in mind in Colossians 2:2-23 and whose doctrine already showed signs of what later would be called Gnosticism.

It is obvious here that the doctrine of these teachers refers to a particular form of Judaism (circumcision; 2:11-13; dietary observances, celebration of yearly, monthly and sabbatical holy days, 2:16; the Mosaic law as a foundation for everything, 2:14, 17). But it is no less certain that we are dealing with a more or less heterodox and syncretistic Judaism. And in my opinion those authors are correct who see here various traits of what were later to appear as peculiar to Gnosis. In fact these teachers follow a human "philosophy" (2:8), took pleasure in "worshipping angels" (2:18), they affect a reputation for "religious" wisdom-*sophia* and humility through a rigorous asceticism involving all kinds of food ("Do not handle, Do not taste, Do not touch") "in severity to the body" (*en apheideia tou somatos*, 2:22-23). An affectation of superior wisdom, the exaggeration of the importance of angels as intermediary beings between God and the world, the tendency towards an exaggerated scorn for the body, are all traits that when overemphasized will be characteristic of Gnosticism.[1]

That we are dealing in the teaching of these false "doctors" of Colossae with certain "Gnostic" characteristics can be further argued from the way in which St. Paul expresses his aim, which is to forearm the Colossians and to fortify their hearts against these false doctrines. He wishes to lead them to "all the riches of an assured understanding (*suneseos*) and the knowledge (*epignosis*) of God's mystery, of Christ, in whom are hid all the treasures of wisdom (*sophias*) and knowledge (*gnoseos*)" (2:2-3). Paul then expresses his purpose in terms of a true wisdom and a true *gnosis* which are opposed to false wisdom and a false and quite human "philosophy."

To return to our original point, then, we may quite naturally assume that in opposing these false teachers who boasted about their "severity to the body," St. Paul wished intentionally to state as a characteristic of true *gnosis* the fact that in Christ,

---

1. Insofar as we can know what it was, we can see the syncretistic Jewish-Gnostic position of Cerinthus. See, for example, A. E. Brooke, **The Johannine Epistles** (ICC, Edinburgy, 1948), pp. 45-49.

and principally in Christ glorified, the fullness of divinity dwells "bodily."

However, the struggle between the spiritualistic-dualistic mentality and the concreteness of the Bible in the area of Christology, hinted at in the Epistle to the Colossians, comes into its own in the Epistles and Gospel of St. John.

The polemical basis not only of the Epistles but also of St. John's Gospel is generally acknowledged by scholars. They also admit that the ambience presupposed by the Gospel (the faithful to whom it was addressed, the adversaries, its whole problematic) is substantially the same as that of the Epistles.[2]

Furthermore, in order to prove that the adversaries aimed at in the Gospel are substantially the same as those in the Epistles, there is an extrinsic argument which seems decisive to me. Historically, we find from the epistles of Ignatius of Antioch and the letter of Polycarp, that in the year 110 the presupposed situation of John's Epistles in respect to the errors that had spread about in the community was still substantially the same and was developing in the same regions and the same milieu that were John's. We must therefore believe that it came about during the time that lapsed between the Epistles and the Gospel.

One piece of evidence to this effect is that the letter of Polycarp (Philippians 6:3-7:1) speaks of the heretics as "false brothers" who were then living and were dangerous to the Christian community with the same expressions that we find in 1 John 4:2-3; 2 John 7. The heretics Polycarp speaks about must then be the same spoken of by Ignatius.

The ambience presupposed by John's Epistles presupposes the existence of a secession movement that had grown among the Christians (1 John 2:19) as a result of the propaganda of some people and the spread of false doctrines. For these

---

2. See, for example, E. Hoskyns, **The Fourth Gospel** (London, 1947), pp. 48-57.

"antichrists" (1 John 2:18) Jesus is not the Messiah nor the Son of God (*ibid.* 2:22-23; 4:15; 5:1 and 5; 5:10-12).

They did not deny Jesus' messiahship in the sense the Jews did. In John we find no trace of that preoccupation to demonstrate that Jesus is the Messiah announced by the prophets as we do in Matthew, for example. The denial that Jesus was the Christ had another meaning for them.

For them, the later denial that Jesus was the Son of God bore more exactly upon the fact that Jesus was the Son of God incarnate (*ibid.* 4:2; 2 John 7). They denied the redemptive value of Jesus' death on the cross and admitted the importance only of his baptism in water (1 John 5:6-12). These same men styled themselves as prophets and spiritual men (*ibid.* 4:1).

It seems hard not to recognize in these characteristics the position of Cerinthus as given to us by Irenaeus, or at least theses that are quite close to his. He said that Jesus was a holy man but merely a man. At the moment of his baptism Christ descended, not God, but an aeon of a Gnostic type. He then maintained that this Christ operated through the life of Jesus, announced the good news and worked miracles, but at the moment of his passion he left him again. The one who died and rose again was the pure man Jesus, not the Christ because he was impassible.[3]

Therefore, for Cerinthus, the whole work of our salvation was not the work of Jesus, but of the aeon Christ and was limited to the time in Jesus' life between his baptism and passion exclusively. This work was basically limited to the proclamation of doctrine.

The pivotal point of this error, which St. John is combatting, was obviously the denial of the essential and actual historical importance of the *sarx* and *aima* of Jesus in his person and in his work for us, within the pretext of a more prophetic and more spiritual vision of Christianity.

---

3. See, for example, A. E. Brooke, **loc. cit.**

At its root was an excessive spiritualism. The error touched the very essence of the apostolic message, which is that Jesus of Nazareth, a true flesh and bone man like ourselves, with the exception of sin, is the Christ, the Savior, and the Son of God incarnate.

John is deeply concerned with warning the faithful against the dangers of this error. And he does so with consummate force and an almost unpolished directness. The characteristic themes from the Epistles and those carefully selected and explicated themes from the Gospel on the life of Jesus and from his discourses have this specific purpose.[4]

As for the importance of the *sarx* in Jesus' person and the fact that Jesus is the Son of God, although completely man as we are (i.e. the unity between Jesus, the Christ and the Son of God), the Epistles tell us: "By this you know the Spirit of God: every spirit which confesses that Jesus Christ has come in the flesh is of God" (1 John 4:2); and "For many deceivers have gone out into the world, men who will not acknowledge the coming of Jesus Christ in the flesh; such a one is the deceiver and the antichrist" (2 John 7).

The Gospel has the well known statement which seems paradoxical at first sight: "the Word was God . . . and the Word became flesh" (John 1:1-14). Obviously, "flesh" here means man. But precisely in this context, the evangelist can speak of man with the word "flesh" because in his biblical notion of man the "flesh" is in the foreground of its view and expression of man. Flesh means man; the notion begins with the flesh in order precisely to point up the essentiality of the flesh in this particular man.

Therefore *Verbum caro factum est* is the supreme expression of the indissoluble relations which by God's will exist between corporeity and salvation in the Christian perspective. We

---

4. See John 20:30, 31.

have come very far from the disincarnate spiritualism of the Greek tradition.

2) *Corporeity and the work of redemption in Jesus' earthly life*

For the New Testament the incarnation in God's plan was ordered to the redemption through Christ's physical death upon the cross. The true death of the Son of God on the cross is no less essential in God's plan according to the Bible than his true incarnation.

Paul characterizes the meaning of the incarnation in this way: "For God has done what the law, weakened by the flesh, could not do: sending his own Son in the likeness of sinful flesh and for sin, he condemned sin in the flesh, in order that the just requirement of the law might be fulfilled in us, who walk not according to the flesh but according to the Spirit" (Romans 8:3-4). The sense is this: in sending his Son, a real flesh and bone man except for sin (for which he was to die and rise again), God conquered sin and make it possible for men, even though they were "in the flesh," to live the new divine life. This is something that the Mosaic law of itself was unable to do.

Both the incarnation and the redemption through the death on the cross are unthinkable without the body of Christ. This body (this flesh and blood) is the place where the drama of our salvation unfolds. In and through this body men's reconciliation with God takes place; men were estranged through sin, and now have been sanctified (Colossians 1:21-22). In and through this body comes our redemption from sin (Ephesians 1:7), our purchase by God (1 Corinthians 6:20; see 7:23 and Revelation 5:9), our liberation from the Mosaic law (Romans 7:4; Colossians 2:14), our emancipation from the domination of the principalities and the powers (Colossians 2:15), the reconciliation of the pagans with the Jews (Ephesians 2:16), the reconciliation of all things "for in him all the fullness of God was pleased to dwell, and through him to reconcile to himself all things, whether on earth or in heaven, making peace by the blood of his cross" (Colossians 1:19-20).

In this last idea we have an expression of the cosmic value and as it were the cosmic dimension of Christ's body and the redemption that came about through it, in perfect harmony with Pauline anthropology which, as we have explained, looks upon man's body as the bond of cosmic unity (Romans 8:19-22).

The same idea of the incarnation ordered to the redemption through the death on the cross is echoed in the Epistle to the Hebrews (2:10-18). But the author speaks from a much more highly developed Greek background and is already aware of the distinction betwen the metaphysical level of absolute necessity and the necessarily contingent level of history. He points out how *fitting* it was that once the salvation of man was decided upon, God should make it a reality himself by means of the incarnation and the death on the cross, precisely because those who were to be saved were men of flesh and bone. This is the first time that so valuable an analysis of this type appears in the New Testament: "For it was fitting that he, for whom and by whom all things exist, in bringing many sons to glory, should make the pioneer of their salvation perfect through suffering. For he who sanctifies and those who are sanctified have all one origin. That is why he is not ashamed to call them brethren. . . . Since therefore the children share in flesh and blood, he himself likewise partook of the same nature, that through death he might destroy him who has the power of death, that is, the devil, and deliver all those who through fear of death were subject to lifelong bondage. For surely it is not with angels that he is concerned but with the descendents of Abraham. Therefore he had to be made like his brethren in every respect, so that he might become a merciful and faithful high priest in the service of God, to make expiation for the sins of the people. For because he himself has suffered and been tempted, he is able to help those who are tempted."

It is quite natural then that no less than St. Paul or St. John, the author of the Epistle to the Hebrews insists on stressing the role of the body of Christ in our redemption: "we have been sanctified through the offering of the body of Jesus Christ once for all" (10:10).

In all of this there is nothing particularly extraordinary, since the idea had been clearly expressed in Jesus' words at the institution of the Eucharist, where, as all witnesses agree, he spoke of the blood of the covenant, or of the New Covenant in his blood shed for men; and, according to Paul and Luke, also of his body (given) for them (Matthew 26:28; Mark 14:24; Luke 22:19-20; 1 Corinthians 11:24-25).

The co-essentiality of the body and the blood in the work of redemption was accentuated in the words of institution by his reference to the sacrifice of the cross, the sacrifice of the covenant on Sinai in the blood of the victim, and the sacrifice of expiation in the blood of a goat.[5]

All of this is rather far from the mentality of spiritualistic dualism. On the other hand, this dualism was quite clearly manifest in the error combatted by St. John, which logically denied the essential function of the *sarx* in Christ not only in the incarnation but also in the work of the redemption of mankind. In fact, as we have already stated, it did not grant any redemptive value to Jesus' death on the cross, and looked upon this as the death of a mere man. It valued only the preaching of Jesus after the aeon Christ had descended upon him at the moment of his baptism. Against this error John insists: "Who is it that overcomes the world but he who believes that Jesus is the Son of God? This is he who came by water and blood, Jesus Christ, not with the water only but with the water and the blood" (1 John 5:5).

---

5. See Exodus 24:9 and the aforementioned texts on the institution of the Eucharist; Leviticus 16:16-19; Romans 3:25; Hebrews 9, the whole chapter.

Here we have a polemical statement of the identity between Jesus, the Christ and the Son of God, and of the essentiality for our redemption of the death on the cross with the shedding of the blood of this Jesus Christ, the Son of God.

3) *Christ's permanent and universal mediation*

A fundamental canon of the New Testament is the doctrine of the universal mediation of the man Jesus (1 Timothy, 2:5; Hebrews 8:6; 9:15; Acts 4:12). This mediation is universal in the sense that since Adam's sin all men depend on him, at the very least because he cancelled once and for all the debt for their sin by dying upon the cross for all men.

But this mediation is also lasting, and permanent. In fact, not only did the Son of God incarnate effect this mediation once and for all on the cross for every man, but since he lives forever, he still carries it on for all men after his death. And this is not only because he intercedes on their behalf with God (Hebrews 7:25; 1 John 2:1), but also and especially because by God's will it is he alone who continually transmits to men the divine life, the Holy Spirit: the divine life and the Holy Spirit with which he is filled (Colossians 1:19-20; 2:9-19; Ephesians 2:21-22; John 1:14 and 16).

Especially after the resurrection, Jesus of Nazareth is indeed the life-giving Spirit (1 Corinthians 15:45; 15:22) which means a concrete being that lives by the power of the Holy Spirit and gives life to all, a spiritual life particularly (Ephesians 2:5), but not solely. Therefore "as the Father raises the dead and gives them life, so also the Son gives life to whom he will.... For as the Father has life in himself, so has he granted the Son also to have life in himself, and has given him authority to execute judgment, because he is the Son of man" (John 5:21, 26-27). "Life" here must be understood in the broad sense in which John takes the word: a spiritual, divine life which in its ultimate effects is also physical.

"Jesus Christ," mediator of the New Covenant "is the same yesterday and today and forever"; this synthetic formula from the Epistle to the Hebrews (13:18) takes on its full strength in this context.

This continual action of Christ, the life-giving Spirit, tends to transform us ever more perfectly into his likeness (Romans 8:29), because "we all, with unveiled face, beholding the glory of the Lord, are being changed into his likeness from one degree of glory to another; for this comes from the Lord who is the Spirit" (2 Corinthians 3:18). The ultimate result will be the glorious transformation of our body into a likeness of his glorious body (Philippians 3:10, 20-21).

The whole teaching of the New Testament on Christ *Kyrios* includes among other things also this perspective in which his universal and continual mediation is asserted as not only an intercessory mediation but also one that is a communication of divine life.

To those asking the reason for this state of affairs the New Testament has but one answer, the only possible answer: God freely deigned so to establish it from all eternity. This is the fundamental doctrine of the *eudokia* of the Father, to will from all eternity that all be saved in Christ.[6]

We can never repeat too much that it is this doctrine of the universal and permanent mediation of the man Jesus, Son of God incarnate, communicating the divine life to men, that constitutes the one truly specific characteristic of the Christian religion, in comparison with any other religion or doctrine. This is its true and indestructible force. It would be most unfortunate if in their attitude or action Christians came to overlook it. They would be presenting to the world an adulterated message which the world might well receive but without thereby becoming Christian.

The doctrines of the divine paternity or of charity are not

---

6. See, for example, a synthetic expression of this in **Ephesians** 1-3.

properly speaking peculiar to Christianity unless they are understood and presented in the light of the doctrine of the universal and permanent mediation of Christ in the communication of the divine life to men.

Absolutely speaking, the reason for this is that it is not proper to Christianity to say that God is the Father, but to say that he is the Father of our Lord Jesus Christ, and our Father in Christ. Nor is it proper to Christianity to say that God loves us and we must love him and love one another. Christianity states that he has loved us and does love us in Christ Jesus and we must love him in Christ Jesus and in this same Christ we must love one another.

4) *Jesus' corporeity in his work of mediation and communication of the divine life to the world after his resurrection*

This doctrine of Christ's continual mediation brings us straight to the core of the subject that we wish to treat, for it is from this fact of the universal and permanent mediation of Christ in communicating the divine life to the world that we can understand the importance of the word *permanent* which the New Testament applies to Jesus' body even beyond the Lord's earthly life.

The statement that in Jesus' earthly life his body was co-essential to his person and co-active in his work of our salvation is so natural to the perspective in which the Bible conceives man that it has the value of a general principle. It is a principle that is not limited only to the Lord's earthly life but extends connaturally into his life beyond death.

We therefore have a clear and specific statement of the doctrine that after his death, and even particularly after his death, Jesus continues to communicate his life to the world as the one and universal mediator. We must add that according to the New Testament, in Jesus' new state after death and in his new work, the Lord's body, taking into consideration its glorious state, continues to play the same role that the body in general has in the person and activity of a man.

For the New Testament, this is something that is both natural and necessary. This is the sense of its argument: 1.) we presuppose the biblical view of man that we have explained above, and 2.) the positive will of the Father that we have salvation from a man who alone in his person continually communicates to the world the divine life with which he was filled; 3.) we accept, furthermore, that God established that this man, in all save sin, was and remains true man like us and acts as a true man as we do; 4.) it therefore follows that on the plane of history in the entire salvific action of the mediator, even in its post-earthly phase, the body was to have a co-essential role.

And it is for this reason and within this precise perspective that the resurrection of Christ has a soteriological value in the New Testament. It appears as *necessary* for our salvation (Luke 24:46; 1 Corinthians 15:17). It is necessary not only as Jesus' reward for having suffered death, nor only as a valuable argument for confirming men's faith in the truth of his teaching and in his mission as a special and truly accredited envoy from God, but especially because the world could and can continue to receive the divine life (salvation is nothing else but this!) in this uniqe manner established by God, i.e. by means of a man and including his body.

This unique mode of salvation was that the man Jesus, body and soul, Son of God incarnate, had in his humiliated state to subject himself to suffering and death — the consequences of sin — to atone for sin on the cross, to merit glory for himself and also for his body, and to rise from the dead and continue to communicate the divine life to others in his glorious state which still includes the body.

In all these phases of his history, Christ was to be the "life-giving Spirit," or in other words, a concrete body-and-soul being, penetrated by and living totally in the divine life, the Holy Spirit, which at the same time he communicates to others through his whole being, both body and soul. As head of the Body and also man, Christ therefore continually causes the divine life to flow into the members of the Body, and makes each one, according to the gifts destined for him by God, grow to the full and perfect stature of the Body.[7]

In a real sense, Christ does this from the first moment of the incarnation, but in a plenary sense, only from the moment of his resurrection. Actually, even though he was the Word made flesh, the body of Christ was not totally penetrated with the divine life because he was in a state of humiliation, subject to all the limitations of mortal life, including corruptibility and death which are the consequences of sin. In becoming incarnate Christ submitted himself to these things and accepted to yield in some way to the sphere of sin (Romans 8:3-4; 2 Corinthians 5:21) in order to destroy sin in others by meriting God's pardon for all. By doing this, on his own merit he cancelled the consequences of sin in himself and acquired the right to the glorious resurrection.

From the moment of his resurrection, his body was totally penetrated by the divine life to the point of its connatural glorious transformation.

From now on it is "the glorious body" (Philippians 3:21). Christ, body and soul, is now established as the glorious *Kyrios* in the total and permanent exercise of his prerogatives as Son: "designated Son of God in power according to the Spirit of holiness by his resurrection from the dead" (Romans 1:3).

If through as impossible hypothesis, the man Jesus had only atoned for sin by dying on the cross and had not risen, how could he have been able after his death to communicate the divine life to others in that unique way in which it was to have been communicated according to God's plans i.e. by a true, integral and perfect man, which, of course, involved the body as well as the soul?

---

7. Colossians 2:19. See also Ephesians 4:15, 16; 2:23.

In this case this divine life would in fact not have reached men. They would still not be "saved" by that *soteria* intended by Scripture and God's plan would once again have failed.

This, thèn, is why the New Testament does not separate Christ's death from his resurrection. It either considers death and resurrection in themselves or in relationship to Christ (Philippians 2:6-11; Romans 1:3-4; 8:34) or as they relate to us (2 Corinthians 5:14-21; Romans 4:24-8, 39; 14:9; Philippians 3:7-24; Colossians 2:6-14; 1 Peter 1:1-2:10; 3:13-4:19; 2 Corinthians 4:7-5:15) or again in reference to the whole cosmos (Romans 8:9-23; 2 Peter 3:13).

In the New Testament, the word pair "death-life" or "death-resurrection," whether in us, in Christ or in the cosmos, not only includes the body and the soul but is inseparable in its terms. It constitutes but one process and one mystery. This is the basis outside of which it is impossible to understand the paschal mystery in the sense and the extension that it takes on in the New Testament and in the ancient tradition of the Church as well as in the liturgy.[8]

---

8. See my article "Riflessioni sul senso teologico del mistero pasquale" in **Rivista di pastorale liturgica** 2 (1964), pp. 102-112.

IV

THE PHYSICAL BODY AND MYSTICAL BODY OF CHRIST IN THE NEW TESTAMENT

What we have explained about Christology and corporeity enables us to understand why, according to the New Testament, no salvation or sanctification can be obtained without reference to the physical body of Christ which was born, suffered and died, but which is now glorious and the co-essential principle in the communication of the divine life that he makes to the world.

In other words, the mystical body of Christ is not constituted, nor does it live or develop without being related to his physical body.[1]

---

1. The exegetes are beginning, at least in regard to the theology of St. Paul, to give consideration to this fact in the texts of St. Paul and St. John. See: L. Cerfaux, **La théologie de l'Église suivant saint Paul** (Paris, 1948), pp. 201-215, **ibid. Le Christ dans la théologie de saint Paul** (Paris, 1951), pp. 264-268. S. Lyonnet, introduction and notes to the Epistle to the Romans in the **Bible de Jérusalem** (Paris, 1953), pp. 55-57 and p. 95 note a, b of Romans 8:2. P. Benoit, "Corps, tête, plérôme dans les épîtres de la captivité," in **Revue Biblique** 63 (1956), 15-44.

1) *Faith, Christ's physical body and salvation*

In order for it to obtain its salvific effect, this relationship must come about both in faith and in partaking of the sacraments, most especially baptism and the Eucharist. This is a participation which necessarily also implies the participation of our own bodies since the sacraments are also external and social rites. We now can begin to glimpse how in the New Testament corporeity is in some way the pivotal point upon which, in the wisdom of God's plan, the communication of the divine life to us through Christ, the one mediator, is hinged.

At first sight, this might seem to be a theological construct rather than the conclusion of exegetical analysis. But this is not the case.

In the New Testament, the faith that saves always includes faith in Christ, in his name. This always involves a belief in what Christ is for us and for the world, in his person and his work, according to God's positive will.

In fact, when the New Testament outlines what we must believe about Christ in order to be saved it states precisely: Son of God incarnate (1 John 4:15; 5:5-10), who died and rose for us (Romans 3:22-25; 10:9; Colossians 2:12). The synthetic formulas of christological faith indicate in summary the whole history of Christ in its essential points: pre-existence, incarnation, death and resurrection and the full and glorious exercise of his power (Romans 1:4; 8:32-34; Philippians 2:5-11; Colossians 1:13-20; Ephesians 1:18-23; 1 Timothy 3:16; 2 Timothy 1:9-10; Hebrews 1:2-4; 2:9).

Therefore salvific faith is always connected with the physical body of Christ who was born, rose again and is now in the glorious state of *Kyrios*. When we say that there is no salvation without faith, that faith builds and sustains the life of the mystical Body, we are saying that there is no salvation or mystical Body without being related to the physical body of Christ.

It is true, neverthelss, that from our point of view this relationship in the faith is psychological and spiritual.

2) *Baptism, the physical body and the mystical body of Christ*

According to the New Testament, faith alone does not produce salvation without the sacraments, especially baptism. This does not mean, however, that faith and baptism constitute two means or ways of salvation. They are one unique means, one unique way which is bound up with an interior disposition that must be expressed and manifested in a rite that is also external, or to put it differently, a way that is bound up with an external rite which presupposes an interior disposition for its goal to be achieved (Matthew 28:19-20; Mark 16:16; Acts 2:38-41. See also Acts 8:37 at least as evidence of the ancient tradition of the Church; 16:30-34; Ephesians 4:6).

The Church as the mystical Body of Christ is built up in a special way in baptism (1 Corinthians 12:13; Galatians 3:27-28; Ephesians 4:4-5; 5:25-27; Titus 3:5). According to St. Paul's theology, baptism takes on its meaning in reference to the death and resurrection of Christ, and therefore to the physical body of the dying and rising Christ.

This is a communication and a participation given to our concrete persons, body and soul, of the process of death and resurrection that came about in Christ's physical body. In Christ this process was not a mere physiological phenomenon as death and life might seem to the biologist or philosopher when considered merely in the light of their own scientific principles. It was a religious event, the decisive point in world history, in the struggle between the divine life and its contrary principle, involving both bodies and souls. It is a reality, therefore, which through the physical body of Christ in which it takes place can be bestowed and communicated by God to others. This is precisely what God does in baptism, presupposing the disposition of faith.

It is in this way that the celebration in faith of the symbolic rite of baptism puts our concrete persons, body and soul, in contact with the physical body of the dying and rising Christ, who bestows on us the religious reality of the transition from death to life that he once experienced; in its full maturity it is brought to full fruition in all of us.

This contact that takes place in baptism between the person of the baptized, including his body, and the person of Christ, again including his once dying but now gloriously risen physical body, is not only of a moral order involving an affective remembrance, but of an order that is much more real.

It is a contact of power. And in order to distinguish it from a merely moral and psychological contact, it must be called physical, although its nature is quite special and supernatural. We therefore say that it is a sacramental and mystical contact that brings about between our persons, body and soul, and the person of Christ, body, soul and divinity, a union that is not only psychological, but real. It is of an ontological order that is supernatural and mysterious, which for this reason we call mystical.

By means of this mystical union of ours in baptism with the physical body of Christ and through it with his whole person, soul and divinity — the physical body of the *Kyrios,* who as our Head and source pours the divine life of which he is full into all men — the mystical body, the Church becomes a reality, and is expressed and manifested in that same body.

This is the teaching of Romans 6:3-6; Colossians 2:9-15, 19, which is further enlarged upon in some aspects by Ephesians 2:21; 4:15-16. We find its most synthetic expression in Colossians, and it will be enough for us to use this as our focal point, complementing in liberally with Romans and Philippians.

1. The first point is that in Christ, especially after his resurrection, "the whole fullness of deity dwells bodily" (v. 9). This involves his body which, together with his soul, is filled

to overflowing with the divine power that works in the world, which makes the concrete man, Jesus, body and soul, superior to every creature.

2. From him, as the Head and source, the divine life is bestowed upon us to the point of entirely filling us: "and you have come to fullness of life in him, who is the head of all rule and authority" (v. 10). This idea is re-stated by St. John: "And the Word became flesh and dwelt among us, full of grace and truth. . . . And from his fullness have we all received, grace upon grace" (John 1:14, 16).

3. This communication of divine life by Christ to us comes radically in baptism. In it, to the point of being ontologically transformed into the likeness of the dead and risen Christ, we participate in the death-life process that took place in the physical body of Christ. Thus in baptism we are "buried" with Christ, "also raised with him" (v. 12) and "made alive together with him" (v. 13).

The Epistle to the Romans adds some particulars. Baptism is a baptism *eis Christon*, or in other words, as we see from the whole context, a baptism that consecrates us to him, makes us like him, dependent upon him and under his influence. More precisely it is a baptism *eis ton thanaton* of Christ (Romans 6:3-4). "We were therefore buried with him by baptism into death" (vv. 4-8), and "we have been united to him in a death like his" (v. 5) or, as the passage might otherwise be translated: "we have become one being with him in virtue of a death like his." Therefore "our old self was crucified with him so that the sinful body might be destroyed" (v. 6).

If baptism is an assimilation to the dying Christ, it is also an assimilation to the risen Christ. It communicates Christ's life to us so that we may have our life from his (v. 4) and finally arrive with him at the glorious resurrection of the body (vv. 5, 9, 10).

In order for this to happen, faith is also required (Colossians 2:12).

4. In this process Christ is the head and the fontal source

that transmits the influx of life (Colossians 2:19; Ephesians 4:15-16).

5. This process continues throughout the faithful's whole life. Baptism is only its beginning. It is merely the beginning point from which to grow and connaturally to reach maturity (Colossians 2:19; Ephesians 4:15-16).

An indispensable condition of salvation is therefore to remain ever united with this Head-Source (*ibid.*). "Not holding fast to the Head" (Colossians 2:19) means to separate one's self from life.

6. This same process does not only unite those individuals with Christ who are assimilating themselves to him, but it also unites them to one another in a special unity that makes them one "Body of Christ" that is the Church (Colossians 2:19; Ephesians 4:14-16; 1 Corinthians 12:13).

7. In God's established manner of communicating salvation to men, the physical body of Christ is the pivotal point of contact between God and the world. It is in this reference to and this mystical though real sacramental contact with the death-life process that took place in Christ's physical body (and therefore in reference to and in sacramental contact with this physical body itself) that Christians are assimilated to the *Kyrios,* share in the unique flow of divine life that comes from him, and become a unity among themselves which is the mystical Body of Christ, the Church.

This doctrine is certain even if we do not wish to admit the exegesis of Cerfaux and others[2] who see it explicitly stated in 1 Corinthians 12:13. Where others translate this passage as follows: "indeed we were all baptized in one Spirit to form one body (the Church)," these authors feel that it should be translated differently: "For by one Spirit we were all baptized in one body (i.e. the physical body of Christ) . . . and all were made to drink of one Spirit."

---

2. **La théologie de l'Église suivant saint Paul,** 1948, pp. 207-210.

This latter translation asserts directly that we become the mystical body of Christ through a sacramental and mystical assimilation to his dead and risen body.

Yet it is certain that in the Epistles to the Colossians (1:18-20; 2:9-15, 19) and to the Ephesians (1:22; 2:15-16) the Church is Christ's mystical Body. Just as the working power of the divinity dwells in a plenary way in Christ's now glorious physical body, so in the Church the totality of the operating divine force in Christ dwells. Through Christ, including his now glorious body, this force is bestowed on men as from their Head and source, and unites them in a mysterious unity with him and with one another, making them his sphere of vital action in the world and his concrete manifestation.

3) *The Eucharist, the physical body and the mystical body of Christ*

The doctrine that the mystical body of Christ becomes a reality only through a real ontological contact (which is sacramental, mystical and includes faith) with the physical body of Christ takes on a still more obvious significance when we are dealing with the Eucharist.

a) In St. Paul

For St. Paul's theology, 1 Corinthians 10:16-20 is a capital text, and particularly the following verse: "The cup of blessing which we bless, is it not a communion (*koinonia*) in the blood of Christ? The bread which we break, is it not a communion in the body of Christ?" This notion of *koinonia* applied to the body and blood of Christ in the Eucharist is somewhat explained by the same St. Paul when he refers to the *koinonia* that in eating the victim of the Old Testament sacrifices the Israelite has with the "altar" of the same sacrifice, i.e. with God himself whom the altar represents. Light is also shed upon this notion when he makes reference to the *koinonia* that the pagans acquired with the demons when they ate the victims sacrificed to them.

In fact, *koinonia* in Greek tradition is a technical term from ritual sacrificial language expressing the idea, common in the history of religions, that in the sacred meal where the sacrificial victim was eaten, or where the food and drink offered to the divinity in the sacrifice was eaten, people acquired a "fellowship" with the divinity itself. This fellowship, in the verifiable opinion of religious historians, can go so far as to imply a certain kinship, or even a kind of identification with the divinity. Beyond this, it was the common notion that the participants acquired a "fellowship" among themselves in the sacred meal.[3]

In the Old Testament the Hebrew word corresponding to *koinonia* is not used, but we do encounter the situation itself, as for example at the sacrifice at the foot of Sinai (Exodus 24:4-8) where the fellowship is signified in the spreading of the blood upon the altar and its being sprinkled over the people, not to mention the banquet of the elders with Yahweh on the mountain that followed the sacrifice (Exodus 24:9-11). And we have not a few other examples.[4]

St. Paul's intention, therefore, was to point up, as a thing that must have been quite familiar to the Corinthians, that the *koinonia* that the Israelite had with God in partaking of the sacrificial meal, or the pagans with the demons when they partook of the meals sacrificed to idols, is verified for Christians in the Eucharist, in regard to Christ, although naturally in a much superior way.

But why does St. Paul speak directly of the *koinonia* in the body and blood of Christ? Certainly above all because of the words Christ himself used: "this is my body," "this is my blood,"

---

3. See W. Eichrodt, **Theologie des alten Testaments,** I (1948), 68-69. **Theol. Wört. z .N.T.** III (1938), 799-800.

4. See Eichrodt, **op. cit.,** pp. 69-70.

words which Christians continued to repeat in the eucharistic rites. But the ultimate motive that explains Christ's expressions at the Last Supper is the biblical notion which we have described above, where *soma* can signify the whole person but as seen as starting with the body, the concrete thing in which the person subsists, is made manifest and comes in contact with others. Thus the Eucharist is a *koinonia* with the whole concrete Christ, but starting with his body broken and his blood shed.

St. Paul, naturally, has in mind Christ's physical body which was born, suffered and died, but is now gloriously risen. It had and still has the particular role in salvation with which we are familiar. Besides the body of Christ that is the Church, Paul knows no other body of Christ than this glorious one (Romans 6:9-10).

In this body and this blood the Eucharist gives *koinonia*.

This *koinonia* is not limited to the mere physical reception of Christ's body and blood. It is also *spiritual*, as is proved by the parallel with the sacrifices of the Old Testament and of the pagans. Indeed, a person who receives this body unworthily eats his own condemnation. And what happens to those who receive it worthily? St. Paul does not say. But for him the opposite of condemnation is righteousness and justification (Romans 5:16-17; 8:3-4). With the Eucharist, we are no longer dealing with that justification that we have in baptism, but rather with a growth of that justification. It is this growth in the divine life with which St. Paul is well acquainted, a growth on the part of baptized persons who remain united with the head and source, Christ, in order to grow in God until the perfect age (Colossians 2:10; Ephesians 4:15-16).

In the same context of the Epistle to the Corinthians, there is on the other hand, a direct emphasis on the social effect of the Eucharist which is the *koinonia* among the faithful who are partaking of it. They form one "body" since all are partaking of the same bread (v. 17).

b) In St. John

With St. John this relationship between the physical body of Christ and the Eucharist as the transmission of divine life to us is markedly more developed. This is the result of the polemical tone of the Epistles and the Gospel, about which we have already spoken, directed against an error whose cardinal point was the misunderstanding of the essential function of the *sarx* and *aima* of Jesus in the work of our salvation. As we mentioned this was the product of an exaggerated Gnostic-type spiritualism.

St. John was not merely content with stressing this essential function of the *sarx* in the incarnation and in the work of redemption accomplished by Jesus during his earthly life. He also includes the Eucharist in this perspective of the vindication of the essential function of the *sarx* of the Savior in the continual transmission of the divine life to men.

In fact, it seems to us that a eucharistic sense is unavoidable in John 6:53-71, as is the explanation of these verses within the background of John's polemic against the error we mentioned.

At the end of the first century when the Gospel was written, in the Christian contexts to which it was addressed, with their well established eucharistic practice (1 Corinthians 11:23-25; 10:16-22; Matthew 26:26-29 and paral.; Acts 2:42; 20:11), the text must inevitably be taken by everyone in a eucharistic sense. Also militating for this interpretation is the very vivid realism of the text itself (*trogo* – to chew), which is put in still greater relief by the insistency of Jesus and the scandal taken by many of his disciples to the point of leaving him for good after this episode (vv. 60-62). Nor can we interpret verses 63-65 as a mollification of Jesus' language, and its reduction to a purely spiritual and psychological eating in faith and love, for if that were really the meaning he intended to express the whole cause of scandal would have been removed and there would have been no reason for the desertion of the scandalized disciples.

Here are a few convergent indications that militate for this interpretation:

1. John 20:31 gives the explicit criterion followed by the evangelist (among so many other possible ones) in his choice and selection of the "signs" (and the discourses as well) which Jesus performed in the presence of his disciples: "these are written that you may believe that Jesus is the Christ, the Son of God, and that believing you may have life in his name."

This brings us back not only to John 1:1, 14 but also to 1 John 4:2-3; 5:1; 5:5-11, and therefore to the aforementioned spiritualistic Gnostic error. On the other hand it is obvious that John chose these eucharistic statements of Jesus, recorded in John 6:55 ff., with a very specific aim in view, since he dwelt upon them in his account of the institution of the Eucharist. We are therefore led to believe that John 6:53 ff. is following the criterion of choice set down in John 20:31-32 which is that of the polemic against the spiritualistic Gnostic error.

2. Christian tradition, which is directly derived from the words of Jesus in the institution of the Eucharist, in this matter speaks of the "body" of Christ and the "blood of Christ" (1 Corinthians 10:16-17). Yet in the sixth chapter of his Gospel, John never speaks of the body and bood but of the flesh and blood of Christ. Why? This brings us back to John's emphasis on the flesh of Jesus: John 1:14; 1 John 4:2-3; 2 John 7, which, again, are all polemical passages against the Gnostic error that misunderstood the function of the flesh in Jesus and in our salvation.

3. John 6:60, 61, 64, 66 tells us that the scandal of some of the followers of Jesus upon hearing his eucharistic statements was so great that at that very moment: "Many of his disciples drew back and no longer went about with him" (v. 66). And the evangelist warns that "Jesus knew from the first who those were that did not believe" (v. 64).

We have here a marked parallel with 1 John 2:18-28, where

we are told that the spiritualist Gnostics who misunderstood the importance of the *sarx* of Jesus: "went out from us, but they were not of us; for if they had been of us, they would have continued with us; but they went out, that it might be plain that they all are not of us" (v. 19).

We cannot avoid the impression that for the evangelist, what happened with some of Christ's disciples when he made his eucharistic statements was the figure and protoype of what happened at the end of the first century to those who until then had been followers of the Christian community; they were scandalized at the assertions of apostolic tradition about the function of the flesh of Jesus in the plan of salvation, and broke with the community.

The evangelist's mention of the eucharistic scandal experienced by Jesus' disciples was aimed at striking at these first century schismatics.

4. It is true that it does not say in the Epistles that these gnosticizing spiritualists did actually arrive at the logical conclusions of their contempt for the flesh in Jesus by also rejecting the doctrine and practice of the Church with regard to the body and blood of Christ in the Eucharist. But the transition from one denial to the other is so slight and so inevitable that it would not be an arbitrary conjecture to suppose that in fact they had completed the transition by the time John wrote the Gospel; or at least that John was concerned with this particular consequence, which if not yet reached was not long in coming, and that for this reason he reaffirmed the salvific function of the flesh and blood of Christ in the Eucharist from an anti-Gnostic point of view.

That we are not dealing with an arbitrary conjecture is shown by the historical fact that about twelve years after John wrote his Gospel, in the same areas and in the same heretical ambience that he had in mind in the Epistles and the Gospel, this particular anti-eucharistic conclusion made a much more explicit appearance, as Ignatius of Antioch tells us.[5]

5. It is also worth noting the correlation between what John 6:53-59 has to say about the connection between eating the flesh and drinking the blood of Jesus and having or not having in one's self life or eternal life, and what 1 John 5:5-12 (especially vv. 11 and 12) says about the connection between believing and the Son of God's coming not only in water but also in blood, and having or not having in one's self the eternal life that God has given us in the Son. The heretics whom John mentions do not have eternal life in them because they do not have Jesus the Son of God who came in water and the blood. In both cases there is the common idea that eternal life is not present without relationship to the blood (and the flesh) of Jesus; at least a relationship in faith and confession in the Epistle, a relationship of real if sacramental, eating in the Gospel.

This point which the sixth chapter of St. John mentions within the framework of a polemic against the spiritualist Gnostic error that deprived the flesh of Jesus of its essential importance in the process of salvation, seems basic to me for an understanding of the whole import of these texts. In this context a few things come to light:

1. The assertions made by Jesus in John 6:53 on the need to eat his flesh and drink his blood in the Eucharist in order to have life or everlasting life in one's self, take on an incomparable importance when they are seen in the background of the biblical doctrine of the co-essential function of the physical body and in a special way of Jesus' physical body in the accomplishment of salvation.

The institution of the Eucharist therefore is evidently the

---

5. **Smyrn.** VII. Here in this text from Ignatius we note the connection between incarnation, passion, resurrection and Eucharist.

point where, in a free but from God's point of view most wise way, we have a concretization first of all a) of the general principle of the co-essential and *permanent* function of Jesus' body in the transmission to us of the divine life which is then the accomplishment of our salvation: a principle that follows from the fact that the Savior and our one and permanent mediator is the man Jesus Christ, soul and body, with a body that is now glorious; and, secondly, b) a concretization of the other general principle: that in us the concrete man, body and soul, must be saved and cooperate or be impregnated in its own way with the accomplishment of this salvation.

These two principles imply the supreme reasonableness of the fact that in his transmitting the divine life to the world through Christ, God devised a means in which it was possible for every concrete man, body and soul, to come in contact with salvation. But this is not only a psychological contact with the concrete man Jesus, including his body, which was born, suffered and died, and is now in the glorious state. Indeed, the body is the connatural channel of communication of man to man.

This wonderful means was the Eucharist.

2. If I am not mistaken, this context radiates with a brilliant light in John 6:56-57: "He who eats my flesh and drinks my blood abides in me, and I in him. As the living Father sent me, and I live because of the Father, so he who eats me will live because of me."

To eat the flesh of Christ is the same as "eating Christ": the expression "who eats my flesh" of verse 56 is the equivalent of "who eats me" in verse 57.

Eating the flesh of Christ brings about the union between Christ and the person who eats: Christ dwells in him and he in Christ. Here, in terms of a reciprocal abode, John expresses what St. Paul meant in terms of *koinonia*. This reciprocal compenetration includes the transmission of the divine life that fills Christ from the Father and is communicated by Christ to men through the eating of his flesh.

Christ's flesh appears as the living vehicle of the transmission of the divine life from the Father through Christ to the one who eats Christ. This explains why Christ's very flesh, the Word of God made flesh, is completely penetrated with the divine life as is his whole human nature. St. Paul had said that in him dwelt the fullness of divinity *somatikos*. Therefore the flesh is alive with divine life and gives this same life to one who eats it.

Naturally, this comes about only on the supposition of one's proper dispositions: on the condition that we are not eating it to our own condemnation, as St. Paul warned. For his part, in the first part of this sixth chapter as well as in 6:61, 63, 64, 66-69, St. John treats at length the necessity for faith in order for Jesus' promises to be fulfilled in those who eat his flesh.

The phrase from John 6:63: "It is the spirit that gives life, the flesh is of no avail" takes on its connatural significance in this same light. It is not a contradictory denial of what has been said above about the supreme salvific value of Jesus' flesh, but an explanation of this same value in the light of verse 57. Jesus' flesh truly transmits the divine life to the one eating it provided he is animated by faith.

But this does not happen simply because it is flesh. Flesh alone is of no avail in the sphere of the divine life. But when the flesh is compenetrated by the Spirit, i.e. divine life, as is the flesh of the incarnate Word who is the lifegiving Spirit (1 Corinthians 15:45), then it is of some avail.

The doctrine that Jesus can give life to others because he himself is filled with the divine life of the Father, already expressed in a general way in John 1:14, 16, and through the resurrection of the bodies in John 5:26, comes at this point to be applied to the Eucharist.

We have therefore clearly to assert that this doctrine of the physical body of Christ, filled with the divine life as is his whole person, and therefore the indispensable transmitter willed by God of this life (which is both spiritual and corporeal, in the resurrection of the body), for a person who comes

3 The Flesh

in contact with it in faith, is the summit of the theology of the corporeity both of man in general and of Christ in particular, in the biblical perspective.

3. The text of John's Gospel puts no limits on the necessity of eating the flesh of Jesus and drinking his blood in order to have divine life: "Unless you eat the flesh of the Son of man and drink his blood, you have no life in you" (v. 53).

Here we have two problems arising: a) Is the eating of the Eucharist of absolute necessity in order to have divine life? b) Does this include the absolute necessity of communion under both species?

The Gospel text does not resolve these two problems. Their resolution will be the accomplishment of a complete theology of the Eucharist which developed gradually.

In the New Testament view of the theology of the corporeity of man in general and Christ in particular, one thing is certain: Christ's physical body has an essential and universal permanent function in the transmission of the divine life to men.

The doctrine of Christ as the unique and permanent mediator of divine life also includes the notion that there is no transmission of divine life in a world where, in accordance with the manner that befits him, his physical body does not have an essential function in the totality of his person.

Therefore, if Jesus' statement in John; "Unless you eat the flesh of the Son of man and drink his blood, you have no life in you" needs some clarification, this does not mean that in certain cases it will be possible to have this divine life even without relation to the physical body of Christ, as if there were aspects of this transmission where in the totality of Christ's human nature the body of Christ did not have its co-essential function.

Similarly, the New Testament does not resolve the question of the precise relationships between baptism and the Eucharist in respect to our sacramental assimilation to Christ's physical body and the transmission of the divine life by Christ to us.

We shall have to find an explanation in which three facts will be preserved: a) whoever does not eat the flesh of Christ and drink his blood in the Eucharist, does not have divine life; b) the baptized person who has not yet really eaten the Eucharist still has the divine life; c) the moment when we eat the flesh of Christ in the Eucharist is not the only moment at which we receive grace.

V

THE CONTRIBUTION OF PATRISTIC TRADITION

The doctrine of corporeity in its relations with anthropology, Christology, the theology of the sacraments in general and of the Eucharist in particular was too marked in the New Testament for it not to have survived in the consciousness of later tradition.

This does not mean, however, that some of the Fathers and later theologians in both theory and practice did not at times succumb to the temptation of the disincarnate spiritualism of Greek philosophy and Encratism, nor allow themselves to escape every expression of this kind. The well-known evolution of St. Augustine from the Neo-Platonizing spiritualism of the beginning of his conversion to the Christian concreteness which he discovered through his pastoral ministry, can be cited as a significant example.

Even today the temptation of disincarnate spiritualism is not unheard of. The same was all the more true in an age where a more noble philosophy gave rise to the great thought of the ancients and formed the general cultural atmosphere of the times: middle Platonism and Neo-Platonism also showed this particular characteristic.

But it is important to note that biblical thought and the Christian instinct soon dispelled this temptation when it was pointed out to the minds of some of the Fathers and caused their conscious reflection to forcefully combat it.

As was natural, this happened especially at times of polemics against errors that showed only too clearly the harmful consequences of a misunderstanding of the importance of corporeity either in man or in Christ specifically in the way of salvation willed by God.

For our purposes there are five polemics that have particular importance:

1. The polemic of the Fathers against dualism, either in its Docetist form as with Ignatius of Antioch, its developed Gnostic form as with Irenaeus or Tertullian, or in an Encratist form as with Clement of Alexandria.

2. The polemic against those who denied the resurrection, which we find in the Apologetes and the anti-Gnostic Fathers.

We know how unpalatable the dogma of the resurrection of the body was for the Greek mentality. All the Fathers who sought to defend the Christian position on this point developed the theme that man is neither solely a soul nor solely a body, but a composite of both, and therefore when God calls men to salvation he is calling also his body which will rejoin the soul in the last analysis at the resurrection.[1]

3. The anti-Arian polemic. When the Fathers found themselves obliged to explain the relations between the divinity and humanity in Christ they clearified the notion that in the work of salvation Christ's humanity, including his body, was

---

1. See for example: Athenagoras, **De resurr. mortuorum** 15; Justin, **De resurr.** 8; Irenaeus, **Haer.** V 6-7; Tertullian, **De resurr. carnis** 53.

the instrument through which the divinity operated.[2] This notion is most important for an understanding of how Christ's body could have had and still has such importance for us.

4. The polemic against Apollinarianism. To show that Christ is perfect man and that he assumed an integral human nature, the Fathers explained what an integral human nature was. In this context, particularly, we see the relevance of the axiom: the Word did not save what it did not assume.

5. The polemic on the hypostatic union, especially that of Cyril of Alexandria against Nestorius.

Our task here, obviously, is not to exhaust all this material. It will be enough for us to make a few quick soundings, stressing especially those Fathers who in their concern for indicating the importance of corporeity in the Christian perspective, also dealt with the sacramental economy and the Eucharist especially. These will be Ignatius, Irenaeus, Tertullian and Cyril of Alexandria. In this area, Cyril may be considered the summit of patristic thought. From him through St. John Damascene many of the patristic views on the matter concerning us will come to be shared by St. Thomas.

1) *Ignatius of Antioch*

In the letters of St. Ignatius of Antioch St. John's teaching on the *sarx* of Christ, including the eucharistic perspectives from which the evangelist's doctrine flows, is reflected in bright splashes of light. This is all the more true since this bishop had to combat the same adversaries as St. John, who had then become even more dangerous on account of the clearer consequences that they deduced from their teaching and the

---

2. See Th. Tschipke, **Die Menscheit Christi als Heilsorgen der Gottheit** (Freiburg-im-B., 1940).

more striking success of their propaganda, putting in serious peril the very existence of the community of Asia Minor.

By this time their doctrine about Christ was clearly Docetist: his body, nativity and passion were merely apparent. In the area of morality, they abandoned charity.[3]

In prayer and worship, they abandoned the Eucharist and the common prayer of the community and held schismatic meetings. "They held themselves aloof from the Eucharist and from the prayer (of the community) because they did not admit that the Eucharist is the flesh of our Savior Jesus Christ, that the flesh suffered for our sins and that the Father, in his goodness, raised it from the dead."[4]

Ignatius' reaction focuses entirely on the word-pair: *sarx-pneuma*. These two words are understood by him generally from the biblical viewpoint of the New Testament. *Sarx* means the whole man, but beginning with his flesh and blood, his outward self. *Pneuma* means the divine element or aspect which penetrates the whole man and therefore signifies the whole man but beginning with the divine element or aspect which is essentially unattainable to the senses.

Christ is one and not divided. He is *sarx* and *pneuma* at the same time: "One is the physician, flesh and blood, generated and unborn, in the flesh he is God, in death true life, both from Mary and from God, he is first passible and then he cannot suffer, Jesus Christ our Lord."[5] He is "perfect man."[6] One who does not confess him in the flesh (*sarkophoros*), has completely denied him and has become a bearer of death.[7]

---

3. Docetism: see for example, **Smyrn.** 2-7; "They care nothing of charity, nor of the widow, nor of one in trouble, nor of one who is a prisoner or a freeman, nor of one who is hungry or thirsty," **Smyrn.** 6, 2.

4. **Smyrn.,** 7, 1.

5. **Eph.** 7:2. See also **Trall.** 9, 1-2.

6. **Smyrn.** 4, 2.

7. **ibid.,** 5, 2.

We must believe him in the flesh even after the resurrection, "in the *pneuma* united with the Father." The Apostles, after his resurrection, touched him and believed, "holding him to be in his flesh and in his *pneuma*."[8]

Whatever the Docetists may say,[9] we also are "carnal" and not *asomatoi* like the demons.

Our salvation is this: "to remain in Jesus Christ carnally and spiritually — *sarkikos, pneumatikos* —"[10] as Christ himself was, who even though he was in the flesh was *pneumatikos* and united with the Father.

This union in flesh and spirit requires faith and charity: we must believe in the flesh and the spirit of Christ and love his flesh and his spirit with our own flesh and spirit.[11]

To be united to Christ in such a way we must be strong in the doctrine of the Lord and the Apostles and be united and subject in all things to the bishop, as well as united to one another: "Submit to the bishop and to one another, as Christ is subject to the Father according to the flesh and the Apostles to Christ, the Father and the Spirit; *so that the union may be carnal and spiritual*."[12] Only in this way can all that we do prosper *carne et spiritu, fide et caritate, in Filio et Patre et Spiritu*.[13]

We must live a virtuous Christian life.[14] We must participate *sarkikos* in Christ's passion in order to arrive with him at the resurrection.[15]

---

8. **ibid.**, 3, 1-3.

9. **ibid.**, 2.

10. **Eph.** 10:3. See also **Magnes.** 13, 1 and 2; **Smyrn.** 13, 1 and 2; Smyrn. 3, 2; 12, 13. **Rom.** proem.; **Ad Polyc.** 1, 2; 2, 1; 5, 1.

11. **Eph.** 14; **Smyrn.** 12, 13.

12. **Magnes.** 13, 2.

13. **ibid.**, 13, 1.

14. See **Eph.** 10:1-3; 15.

15. **Eph.** 11; 20; **Magnes.** 5, 2; 9, 1-3; 11; **Trall.** proem., 9, 1-2; 10, 1; 11, 2; **Rom.** 6:1-3; 7:2-3; **Phil.** 8:2; **Ad Polyc.** 7, 1.

He praises those who remain in chastity "in honor of the flesh of the Lord."[16]

In a special way we must participate in the Eucharist which is "the flesh of our Savior Jesus Christ, the same that suffered for our sins and which the Father, in his kindness, raised."[17] "Whoever contradicts this gift of God . . . is dead."[18]

In fact the Eucharist is "the remedy of immortality, the antidote for not dying but living in Jesus Christ for ever."[19]

Therefore the necessity "for coming together for the Eucharist and giving glory to God."[20]

But woe to those who form separate groups for worship! Christ's flesh is one, his blood is one, and therefore so much the Eucharist be one: "Be careful therefore to make but one Eucharist. Unique is the flesh of our Lord Jesus Christ, and unique is the cup in having the union of his blood. One is the altar, just as the bishop is one with the presbyterate and the deacons."[21] "Who is outside the altar is deprived of the bread of God."[22]

Here then are Ignatius' key ideas: man is not *asomatos* but *sarkikos*: Christ is perfect man and true God; his flesh and his blood were and are essential to our salvation; therefore as men we must remain in him "carnally and spiritually"; and we must "hold him in his flesh and in his spirit"; both things we do by living in faith and charity, taking part in his passion in order to arrive at his resurrection, and participating in his flesh and blood in the Eucharist, united to the bishop and the community of brethren.

---

16. Ad Polyc. 5:2.
17. Smyrn. 7, 1.
18. ibid.
19. Eph. 20, 2.
20. Eph. 13, 1.
21. Phil. 4. See also Eph. 5, 2; Magnes. 7.
22. Eph. 5, 2.

Once again there are splashes of light given off by a spirit that is not concerned with making theories and systems but rather lives these realities with a supreme realism, like one's most profound being.

His expressions are comprehensible only within the framework of the New Testament teaching on corporeity in relationship to anthropology, Christology and the way of conceiving faith and the sacraments, and particularly the Eucharist. But they are of a crystal clarity in the spirit of biblical and Christian concreteness which is very far from the distincarnate spiritualism of Greek philosophy and Gnosticism.

Does St. Ignatius go further in his thought than what we find in the New Testament? He does, in that within this process of our flesh-and-spirit unity with Christ, a process which is completed in faith, charity and the Eucharist, he assigns an essential place to the bishop and hence to the eucharistic assembly of the community, celebrated around the bishop. Our union with the bishop and our participation together as brothers in the one altar around the bishop or his representative, constitutes in some way part of that carnal and spiritual manner in which we men are to unite ourselves to Christ the perfect man and God, and therefore flesh and spirit. "Submit to the bishop and to one another ... that your union may be carnal and spiritual."[23]

The bishop is bishop *en sarki*;[24] but he is the *typos* of God, the universal bishop whom the "carnal" bishop expresses in himself and makes present.[25]

The authority in the Church and the liturgical meetings constitute part of this life "of flesh and spirit" whereby we come to God.

---

23. Magnes. **13,** 2. See also **ibid.** 13, 1.
24. **Eph.** 1, 3.
25. **Magnes.** 3, 1; 6, 1. 2; 13; **Trall.** 2, 1; 3, 1.

2) *Irenaeus*

This same anti-Dualistic and anti-Gnostic polemic continues with Irenaeus. His theology on this point has been the basis for later developments.

He sums up the essential Gnostic thesis in regard to matter in this way: *salutem solum animarum esse futuram, corpus . . . quoniam a terra sit sumptum, impossibile esse participare salutem.*[26]

He counters this thesis with the position of the Bible and the Church: *Homo . . . temperatio animae et carnis*[27] and therefore like the whole man, *esse carnem participem vitae.*[28]

On a basis of Scripture and the preaching of the Church, Irenaeus abundantly develops the theme of corporeity in relation to the creation, the elevation, the fall, the incarnation, the sacraments and especially the Eucharist, asceticism, and to the final term of salvation.

Therefore, from this viewpoint, he says of the *salus carnis* in connection with the Eucharist: "Since they say that the flesh is corrupt and does not participate in life, what flesh is nourished by the body and blood of the Lord? Therefore, either they change their opinion or stop offering these things. On the contrary, for us, the Eucharist is in conformity with our faith and conforms it. We offer to him what is his own proclaiming unanimously the fellowship and the union of the flesh and the spirit. Just as the bread that comes from the earth, receiving the invocation of God, is no longer common bread, but the Eucharist which has been constituted by two elements, the earthly and the heavenly, so also when our bodies partake

---

26. **Haer.** I, 27, 3.

27. **ibid.**, V 8, 2.

28. **ibid.**, IV 4, 3. On Irenaeus' position see G. Joppich, **Salus carnis** (Münsterschwarzach, 1965).

of the Eucharist, they are no longer corruptible because they have the hope of rising forever.[29]

"Vain are all who scorn God's whole economy, deny the salvation of the flesh and disdain its regeneration, saying that it cannot be receptive of incorruptibility — *dicentes eam capacem non esse incorruptibilitatis.*

"If the flesh is not saved, then neither has the Lord redeemed us by his blood; the cup of the Eucharist is no longer the communion of his blood and the bread we break is not the participation in his body. . . .

"Since we are his members and are nourished on created things . . . he said that this drink from created things is his own blood, which nourishes our blood, and he asserted that this bread, also from created things, is his own body which nourishes our bodies.

"Therefore when the cup and the bread receive the word (*logos*) of God and become Eucharist, the body of Christ with which our own flesh is formed and grows, how can they ever say that our flesh cannot receive God's gift of eternal life, since this flesh has been nourished by the body and blood of the Lord and made a member of the Lord?

In the Epistle to the Ephesians St. Paul says that we are members of his body, of his flesh and bones. He does not say this of some spiritual and invisible man — the spirit has neither flesh nor bone — but he speaks of the make-up of a true man, composed of flesh, nerves and bone, which make-up is nourished with the cup, the blood of the Lord, and augmented by the bread, his body.

"In the fashion in which life's root, placed in the ground, produces fruit in due time, and the seed cast upon the ground and decomposed, reappears multiplied by the Spirit of God which is in all things, and then those elements which in God's

---

29. **ibid.**, IV 18, n. 5.

wisdom come to be used by man, receiving the word of God, become Eucharist in the body and blood of Christ, so also our bodies nourished by this Eucharist, committed to the earth and there decomposed, will rise in time because the Word of God will make them rise for the glory of God the Father."[30]

What is especially remarkable in these texts is the view of cosmic unity which can never be admired enough.

This view of things puts back into place the historical design of salvation, the divine *dispensatio* or *oikonomia,* on all of its levels: lesser creation, man, Christ, divine life in the world.

The pivot of this unity, as a point in which all these levels converge, is man's body, and especially the body of the God-Man. Even if we cannot grasp all of the points in Irenaeus' global vision with equal clarity, the thrust of his thought certainly tends toward the following view of things:

Above all, the lesser creation, made for man,[31] so that it might enable him to achieve his higher goal of divine life,[32] is immediately ordered to man's body.

When the Word formed Adam in the beginning, his utterance was already universal.[33] Therefore, through his incarnation, he "recapitulated" nature as well as the history of man in himself,[34] and took on flesh and blood like us,[35] so that "every thing might see its king, and that in the flesh of our Lord it might see the light of the Father, and that from his flesh rays

---

30. Haer. V 2.

31. Conditio facta est propter hominem: ibid. V 29, 1.

32. Temporalia fecit propter hominem ut maturescens in eis fructificet immortalitatem: ibid. IV 5, 1.

33. In semetipsum fabricator omnium Verbum praefiguravit. ibid. III 22, 3.

34. "Since the first Adam was taken from the earth and was formed by the Word of God, in recapitulating Adam in himself, the Word had to be like him in his birth." ibid., III 21, 10.

35. Et ipse caro et sanguis secundum primaevam plasmationem factus . . . salvans in fine illud quod perierat in principio Adam. ibid. V 14, 1.

might come to us, and therefore man, surrounded by the light of the Father, might achieve incorruption."[36]

The whole work of our salvation is focused upon the *caro* of the Savior, the flesh that sends forth light. Considered in Christ himself, this work came about in the incarnation (which has especial importance for Irenaeus), in the Lord's life and in his passion and death. This salvation reaches us in baptism[37] and in a special way in the Eucharist.

Here, according to Irenaeus, all things are in some way recapitulated, since in the Eucharist the lesser creature of bread and wine is changed through invoking God into the body and blood of Christ in such a way that man can feed on this body and blood and therefore also participate in his own body in that life and incorruption which will reach its fulfillment in the resurrection.

Irenaeus summed up his polemical position against the Gnostics in these words: they contradict *saluti plasmatis Dei, quod quidem est caro: propter quam omnem dispensationem fecisse Filium Dei . . . ostendimus.*[38]

Materiality, corporeity is truly the point of contact of all orders of being — in Christ, even with the divinity — and the salvation of the *caro* through *caro.*

Secondly, in Irenaeus' writings there is the idea that through this whole economy of God there is need to proclaim "concordantly" the possibility and even the fact of the "fellowship and union of the flesh and the spirit": the flesh is "capable of life," in lesser creation, at least when it is used for higher ends, for example in the Eucharist, and in man since, even though man is by nature *temperatio animae et corporis,*[39] this

---

36. Haer. IV 20,2.
37. Corpora enim nostra per lavacrum illam quae est ad incorruptionem unitatem accepterunt ibid. III 17, 2.
38. Ibid., IV Praef. 4.
39. Haer. V 8, 2.

whole *temperatio* including the body can receive the Spirit of God as it does now and did in Adam.[40]

In Christ the whole *vetus plasmatio* of Adam becomes "recapitulated" and penetrated by this Spirit.

Not alone, but in Christ, the whole of creation is in some way compenetrated with the same Spirit. Through the incarnation, the Word "has implanted itself in the whole of creation."[41]

Thirdly, we must underline Irenaeus' supreme realism, and even concretism, which he presents in an eminently biblical perspective. In fact, when analysed in accordance with later developments in eucharistic theology, this realism appears somewhat exaggerated. He says that in the Eucharist the body of Christ nourishes our body and his blood our blood. Strictly speaking, in the Eucharist it is not Christ's body that materially nourishes our body but the eucharistic species under which the body of Christ is present. But we can very well understand what Irenaeus is saying: in the eating of the Eucharist our own body comes into a real and not merely moral contact, a physical contact, even though it is most special and mysterious and therefore sacramental, with the body of Christ. It is through this contact, provided that it comes about in faith and charity, that the whole man, body and soul, is spiritually vivified.

3) *Tertullian*

It is worthy of note that Tertullian's ideas in his anti-Gnostic polemic, specificially in the *Adversus Marcionem* and *De resurrectione carnis,* re-echo those of Irenaeus. Because of this it

---

40. Perfectus autem homo commixtio et adunatio animae adsumentis Spiritum Patris admixta carni. ibid., V 6, 1.

41. In novissimis temporibus homo factus est, in hoc mundo exsistens . . . et in universa conditione infixus. Ibid. V 18, 3.

might seem needless to dwell particularly over what he has to say. Yet it is well known that Tertullian had a special talent for expressing his ideas with particularly precise formulas and rare beauty. For this reason, then, we shall cite here at least two passages from the *De resurrectione carnis*.

The first text is one in which he takes up in his own fashion an idea of Irenaeus in order to impress upon his readers the esteem and the importance that God himself attached to the human body. He speaks of the loving care with which, according to Scripture, God formed Adam's body. Its importance, Tertullian adds, was shown in a special way by the fact that in forming Adam God already had Christ in view, the future incarnation of the Word. "Think again about God, so concerned with and devoted to Adam's body: with his hand, his senses, his activity, his counsel, his wisdom, his providence, and above all his affection that guided his formation of the features. In fact, *in everything that came to be expressed in the human body, there was the light of Christ, the future man, shining through.* For he too was to be clay and flesh and word, and then was earth. So spoke the Father to the Son: let us make man in our image and likeness. And God made man, the very one whom he formed naturally; he made him in the image of God, which is Christ."[42]

The other text contains what seems to me to be the most successful synthetic expression of what we are trying to say in this study: *"caro salutis est cardo."* It is the most felicitous formula, at least when it is understood as including the flesh of Christ (which is more than Tertullian does in the immediate context), and the flesh of Christ primarily.

Caro salutis est cardo: not only instrument, subject, object of salvation, but the pivotal point and hinge of the whole economy of salvation. In synthesis, it is the entire vision of Irenaeus.

---

42. **De resurrect. carnis** 6.

The immediate context of this formula is the following: Tertullian is combatting Dualism, and specifically Docetism. This is the reason for his praise of *caro*: God created it and formed it with such care and love, having the future Christ already in mind; even in natural actions the soul has need of the flesh; in the supernatural area the soul can accomplish its salvation only through and in the flesh; and in a special way this supernatural salvation can be attained only by means of certain rites in which the flesh participates. In addition to the sacraments of baptism, confirmation and the Eucharist, Tertullian names also some rites which we call sacramentals today in the complex ritual of Christian initiation: prebaptismal anointing together with the imposition of the sign of the cross. In these rites the flesh has always an essential part. Finally, there are many things that man must and can do to attain salvation, and they are only accomplished in and through the flesh: asceticism, virginity, martyrdom, etc.

It is in this context that Tertullian exclaimed: *adeo caro salutis est cardo*: how true it is that the flesh is the pivotal point of salvation! Here is the central passage:

"Thus the flesh as the servant and handmaid of the soul is also its consort and co-heir. If this is true of temporal things, why not also of things eternal?

"What I have said up to now about the flesh comes from a consideration of the general state of the human condition.

"We see now, from a Christian point of view, how much God has esteemed this contemptible and gross material.

"It would be sufficient here to realize that absolutely no soul can attain salvation if it does not believe that it is in the flesh: so much is the flesh the pivotal point of salvation.

"When God subjects the soul to himself, it is by means of the flesh that this takes place. In fact, the flesh is washed that the soul might be purified, the flesh is anointed so the soul may be consecrated; the flesh is signed with the mark of the cross so that the soul may be fortified; the flesh is overshadowed by the laying on of hands so that the soul might be illuminated by the Spirit; the flesh is nourished with the body and blood of Christ so that the soul may be nourished by God. These two things which are united in service may not be separated in the reward."[43]

There follows then a further enumeration of these works: virginity, asceticism, martyrdom, etc.

In addition to the credit for having coined the expression: *caro salutis est cardo,* Tertullian in this text has also the merit of having explicitly included in the theological notion of corporeity not only the sacraments, but also what later theology called sacramentals.

In this way, particularly after Ignatius of Antioch's observations on the liturgical celebration of the Christian community around the bishop, the way becomes open for including the entire liturgy within the perspective of *caro salutis est cardo.*

4) *A note on fourth and fifth century Greek tradition*

If we should go from Tertullian immediately to Cyril of Alexandria it is not because there is nothing of special interest to our subject in the intervening Fathers. As a matter of fact in some of them we can find some valuable statements, felicitous synthetic expressions of perspectives that we have already seen in Irenaeus, Ignatius or Tertullian, and even in some aspects a deeper probing into the general doctrine of corporeity.

a) Athanasius

With Athanasius this deeper insight focuses especially on the relations between corporeity, incarnation and our salvation as a "divinization." He had a very clear idea that if anything

---

43. **De resurrect. carnis** 8.

were taken away from the true divine nature of the incarnate Word or from his real and integral human nature, including the human body, our salvation would be destroyed. Here is what he says in *II Contra Arianos* 70 (PG 26, 296): "Never could man have presented himself to the Father if the one who had put on our body had not been the Word of God, truly and by nature. Since we should not have been freed from sin and the curse, without the human flesh that the Word assumed (what would we have had in common with a flesh that would be foreign to us?), man would not have been divinized if the natural, and true Word of the Father had not assumed the flesh. Therefore, union was achieved between the true nature of the divinity and the true nature of humanity in order that salvation and divinization might be assured."

For Athanasius, the fact that the Word assumed human flesh constitutes the pivotal point of our divinization. God became flesh in order to make man godlike through participation. In assuming the flesh, insists Athanasius and many other Fathers after him, he assumed all of mankind in himself.

What is the precise meaning that he attached to this expression? Basically he means merely this: by the fact that the Word was made flesh, lived, suffered, died, and rose in the flesh, every man *by right* can receive in participation his divine nature, his immortality, be born to a new life, overcome every woe including death, rise and be with Christ at his Father's right hand. With Athanasius we have the beginning of the awareness — although many related questions are still undetermined — of the soteriological value of each of the states and events in the life of the Incarnate Word in what he did and suffered in his flesh. Therefore the flesh of the Word appears progressively more as the center of contact and exchange between man and God, even if in its particulars there is not much clarity about the manner in which each man comes to receive this participation in fact, not to say by right, specifically in relation to the Eucharist.

The general principle of this centrality of the flesh can

be found in *III Contra Arianos* (PG 26, 444), 57: "Just as he (the Word) in assuming our body also assumed in himself what is ours, so too we, in receiving him, receive his immortality."

Athanasius' position may be summed up in this text: "If the divine works of the Word had not been accomplished by means of the body, man would not have been divinized. If the Word had not made the weaknesses of the flesh his own, man would never have been liberated.... Since the Word became man and took upon himself the miseries of our flesh, they no longer touch our body, because the Word has come in the body. They have been destroyed by him. Men no longer remain sinners and dead men as a result of their sins, but rising through the power of the Word, they become immortal and incorruptible. When his flesh was born of Mary, the Mother of God, we are told that the one who was born is he who has granted birth and being to others. Consequently, he takes upon himself our birth, and we no longer come back to the earth as earthly beings, but united to the heavenly Word, we are raised to heaven by him. Similarly it is not without reason that he assumed the other conditions of the body. He did so that we might share in everlasting life, insofar as we are no longer mere men, but belong to the Word. We shall no longer die in accordance with our first birth in Adam, but we shall rise from the earth because our birth and all our weaknesses have been transferred to the Word, and the curse inflicted upon us by sin has been taken away by the one who has made himself a curse in us. And rightly so. In fact, insofar as we are of the earth, we die in Adam, we are also brought to life in Christ by being reborn from on high, in water and the Spirit. Henceforth the flesh can no longer be considered earthly because the Word has made himself flesh for us."[44]

Finally, in relation to what we have said above about the

---

44. **III Contra Arianos** 33 PG 26, 393; 396.

works in which we are now engaged, Athanasius says very little about the Eucharist. We might merely wish to point out the following sentence from his second letter to the philosopher Maximus: "We are not deified by participating in the body of an ordinary man, but by receiving the body of the Word himself."[45]

b) Hilarion

In the matter under consideration, Hilarion may be considered as representing Greek tradition. With him we find again the general perpectives of Athanasius.[46]

But with him they have become more perfected because, beyond the generic assertion that every man virtually and by right is assumed by Christ and therefore in some way drawn into the mystery of the Word made flesh, Hilarion specifies more clearly the means whereby this virtual and rightful assumption becomes for every man also an actual and *de facto* assumption to the point of producing its connatural fruits in each individual. These means are baptism, Christian moral life, and especially the Eucharist.

This is what he has to say about baptism and the Christian life, for example: "Because the Word was made flesh . . . we have become reconciled in the body of his flesh. Therefore, through the unity that has come about in the flesh assumed (by the Word), we are in Christ, and this is the sacrament of God hidden for centuries . . . that might be co-heirs, sharing the same body and participating in God's promises with Christ. . . .

---

45. PG 26, 1088.

46. See specifically the generic statement: "He is ignorant completely of life, and totally ignores it, if he does not know that Christ Jesus is true God as well as true man. There is an equal danger in not seeing in Christ either the spiritual element that makes him God or the flesh of our body." **De Trin.** IX 3 PL 10, 282.

"The way to Christ is therefore open to all by means of the union that has come about in his flesh, if they put off the old man and affix him to the cross and . . . in the baptism of Christ they are buried with him in order to rise to life, if in order to enter into and share the union established for them in his flesh, they also place their flesh (on the cross). Christ will transform these bodies in the likeness of his body and will change into the glory, which his flesh now has, the lowliness of those who have been purified by the sacrament of new birth and made conscious that they no longer have their own flesh, but that of Christ."[47] Elsewhere he says "The Sacraments of human salvation (the focus here is on the 'mystery of Christ,' the incarnation) are accomplished in us by giving us life through the power of the sacrament of regeneration in the Father and the Son."[48]

The general idea of these texts is clear: our supernatural life is a process that unfolds in reference to the physical flesh of the incarnate Word, the Word incarnate, dead, risen and now taken to the Father. Hilarion makes a brief allusion to the whole paschal mystery of Christ. From our part the actualization of this process requires baptism and the Christian life. The ultimate stage will be the glorious resurrection of our body in the likeness of the glorious body of Christ.

In reference to the flesh of the incarnate Word, there is an extension in us of the incarnation, death and resurrection of Christ.

The part that has to deal with the Eucharist is magnificently developed by Hilarion. This quasi-extension of the incarnation whereby we as men participate in the divinity of the Word, comes about for each of us especially when we receive the flesh of the incarnate Word in the Eucharist. And this extension to us of the incarnation does not happen on the purely moral

47. In Ps. 91, 9 (PL 9, 499).
48. De Trin. 5, 35 (PL 10, 153).

plane of knowledge and affect, but in a much more real way. Hilarion calls it a "natural way," presupposing the Greek adjective *physikos*. In our terminology we would say that it comes about in a physical way (in contradistinction to a purely moral way), although it is mysterious, in imitation of and remote participation in the union that exists between the human and divine natures in Christ, and therefore the union between the Word and the Father.

Against the opinion of the Arians who in reference to John 17:22 ff. said that between the Word and the Father there exists only a moral union, as between Christ and us, Hilarion stresses that between Christ and us there is not only a moral union, but one that is more "natural," ontological and physical, but also mysterious, as is proved by the union we have with Christ in the Eucharist: "If the Word has truly become flesh and if in the food given to us by the Lord, we truly partake of the Word's flesh, then how can it be said that he is not in us physically, since he was born as man and inseparably united the nature of our flesh to himself, and in the sacrament in which he communicates himself to the flesh he has placed in us his physical flesh in order to raise us to an eternal mode of being? We are therefore *one* because the Father is in Christ, and Christ is in us. Whoever then would deny that the Father is physically in Christ, first denies that we are physically in Christ and Christ physically in us. If then Christ has actually assumed the flesh of our body and the man born of Mary is Christ, and we truly receive him in the mystery of the flesh in his body (and for that reason we will be one with him since the Father is in him and he is in us), how can we assert a union that is solely of the will, while the true physical union (between Christ and us) in the mystery (of the incarnation and the Eucharist), is a sacrament that demonstrates the perfect unity (between Christ, the Father and us)? ... If he wished merely to speak of a unity of the will, why did he speak of a unity of perfect degree and order? He wished us to believe that he is in the Father through the nature of the divinity, that we are in him through his corporeal birth, and he is again in us through the mystery of the sacraments. And thus he wished that we be aware of the perfect unity realized by the Mediator, since we are in him, he in the Father and the Father is also in us, and that in this way we might attain unity with the Father while we are physically in one who is physically in the Father through his natural birth, and that he dwells physically in us. . . . A while before, he asserted the mystery of this perfect unity when he said: *As the Father who lives has sent me and I live through the Father, whoever shall eat my flesh shall live through me.* He lives by means of the Father, and in the manner that he lives through the Father so also shall we live by means of his flesh. . . . This then is the cause of our life, that we who are of flesh have Christ dwelling in us by means of the flesh; and for this reason we live in the way that he lives by means of the Father. . . . We have said all of this because the heretics in order to prove their false doctrine of the solely voluntary unity between the Father and the Son, take the example of our unity with God, as if we were united to the Son and through the Son to the Father only by means of the affective religious will, and as if we had no bond of physical unity with him by means of the sacrament of the flesh and blood. In reality, however, the glory he has given us, the indwelling in the flesh of the Son in us, the corporeal and inseparable union we have with him, shows that we must assert the mystery of a true and physical unity" (*De Trin.* 13-17, PL 10, 246-249).

c) *Others*

We find other felicitous expressions on corporeity and the Eucharist in Cyril of Jerusalem. For example when he says that the participation in the sacred mysteries of the Eucharist make us become *syssomoi* and *synaimoi* (con-corporeal and con-sanguineal) with Christ (*Catech. myst.*, 4, 3). "Thus we become bearers of Christ (*Christophoroi*), since his body and his blood are spread throughout our members. Therefore, according to the blessed Peter, we become "partakers of his divine nature" (*ibid.*). He also says that in the Eucharist the bread and the cup sanctify body and soul: "Just as the bread is akin to the body so does the Word harmonize with the soul" (*ibid.*, no. 5). Finally, we have this text on baptism as a conforming to the physical body of Christ which died and is now in glory: "Baptized and clothed in Christ, you are engrafted on the Son of God. God, who has predestined us to adoption, has made us conforming to the glorious body of Christ. Since you have become sharers with Christ, you may rightly be called christs" (*ibid.* 3, 1).

Gregory of Nyssa has a few passages on the "mystery of the flesh of Christ" which are an expression of a rather perfect synthetic perspective that was later taken up by Cyril of Alexandria. This "mystery of the flesh of Christ" (*Contra Eunom.* V, PG 46, 700) consists in this: that the Son of God has assumed human nature and compenetrated it with life-giving power in order that through it he might lead back fallen man to himself and to immortality. In this process of the mystery of Christ's flesh, the Eucharist, in God's plan, has an essential function. Indeed, "since man is a twofold being, made up of body and soul, it is necessary for those attaining salvation to come in contact by means of that twofold element with the one who is leading them to life. Thus the soul obtains the principle of salvation by clinging to him through faith. In fact to be united with life means to participate in life. On the other hand, the body comes to communion and union with the Savior in a different way.... Having tasted something that unbinds our nature, we must of necessity have need of something that will recompose what has been released, in such a way that this salutary remedy will by its contrary power destroy the damage wrought by the poison that had previously been placed in the body. What is this remedy? Nothing other than that body that showed itself to be stronger than death and which was the principle of our life. As the Apostle tells us, a bit of leaven absorbs the whole; therefore the body, granted immortality by God, placed in our body, changes it and transforms it completely in its image. . . . The immortal body, when it is infused in the one who receives it, transforms it in accordance with its own nature. However, it is not possible for something to enter into the body without blending with its vital organs by means of eating and drinking. Therefore it is necessary that the life-giving power be received in the body in accordance with the manner possible to its nature. This life-giving grace was given only to the body that had received God. . . . This body that had received God . . . sustained itself by bread. And this body, through the indwelling of the Word of God was raised to divine dignity. Therefore we rightly believe that now the bread sanctified by the Word of God is transformed into the body of the Word of God. . . . Because of this, he is infused in all who believe in the economy of grace, by means of the flesh, which maintains itself by bread and wine, and blends with the bodies of the believers, so that man too might share in the incorruptibility of union with the immortal. And this becomes a reality through the transformation of the nature of the sensory elements in this body by means of the *Eulogia*" (*Great catechetical discourse,* c. 37, PG 45, 93 A-97 B). Granting a few less felicitous expressions and a thought which in some of its particulars is still searching, we find quite noteworthy in this text a strong connection (based on the pivotal point of man's body, and specifically that of the Lord) made between anthropology, inferior nature, incarnation and Eucharist. On many points a similar foreshortening of ideas will become the goad and strength of the thought of Cyril of Alexandria.

As for St. John Chrysostom, he is noted for his marked eucharistic realism, and his stress on the background of anthropology in general and specifically the incarnation. In the anthropological sphere, the following passage is of interest. It is taken from the 60th Homily to the Antiochean people (Roman Breviary, Sunday after Corpus Christi, 2nd nocturn): "Because the Word has said 'this is my body,' we assent to it, believe it and contemplate it with the eyes of the spirit. Christ has not given us something that is only sensory: in sensory things, he gave us all things as intelligible. This is also true in baptism: through a sense-object, water, he gave us a gift; the intelligible thing that becomes a reality there is generation and renewal. If you were without a body, he would have given you incorporeal gifts. But since the soul is united to the body, in sensory things he has given you things of the intellect."

For Chrysostom's ideas on the incarnation, we might cite the following text: "Since we were (members of his members and flesh of his flesh) not only by love but also in a real way, we are blended with his very own flesh. . . . Indeed, this comes about through this food he has given us. . . . I wanted (he tells us) to become your brother. For you I have participated in flesh and blood. He gave you back this same flesh and blood through which he becames your kinsman" (*In Jo. Hom.* 46, no. 3, PG 59, 260).

We can frankly say, however, that all of these various aspects of the thought of this period culminate with St. Cyril of Alexandria, who has given us a much finer and more finished synthesis.

5) *Cyril of Alexandria*

Even before the controversy with Nestorius, St. Cyril of Alexandria was completely absorbed with a consideration of the incarnation and its connections with the Eucharist. In this he kept to the wake of the preceding Fathers, specifically Athanasius, whom he accurately and constantly read, and was spurred on by the intense vision of the unity of Christ himself and of the whole Christian economy, pivoted precisely in the flesh of Christ, as the flesh of the incarnate Word.

This was the reason for his vehement reaction against the dualism of the Nestorians with its excessive separation of the human and divine natures in Christ.

Nestorius' position, at least as Cyril interpreted it, denied that the humanity assumed by the Word (including the body) was assumed by him in such a way that from the first instant of his existence it was always a humanity proper to the Word; he asserted that on the contrary, this was a humanity of someone other than the Word, merely united to him by a moral bond and by grace.

Such a theory sundered Christ's unity and deprived his humanity, specifically his body, of the function of physical and not merely moral mediation that was both universal and lasting, as well as of its pivotal function of physical contact between God and men, and the center of cosmic unity.

In a special way, it changed the whole complection of the eucharistic sacrifice and the Eucharist in the economy of salvation. In fact, the logic of this system, Cyril observed, would be to say that in the Eucharist we do not receive the Word's own body, but that of someone else, which has merely been sanctified by the Word and united morally to him. In this case, Cyril points out, the Eucharist would be completely useless, and mere anthropophagy.[49]

To this view, Cyril opposes the folowing assertions, brought together into a whole system of undeniable magnificence, in which, along with the basic notions of St. John, we find the confluence of the best of the preceding tradition, especially Athanasius, in what it had to say about corporeity, incarnation, Eucharist and our salvation.

He starts with the basic principle that the Word did not only assume integral human nature, specifically the flesh, but that he *became* flesh. The flesh he assumed is the flesh belonging to the Word of God. The Word is life because the Word is from the Father who is the origin of all life. Therefore the

---

49. **Anathema** 11 (aproved with the rest at the council of Ephesus) and Cyril's explanations. Cfr. for example: **Explanations of the eleven chapters** (PG 76, 312), **Ep. 17** to Nestorius (PG 77, 113-116), **Five books against Nestorius** IV, 4-5 (PG 76, 189-97).

flesh of the Word is the flesh of life: vivified, the source of life, and life-giving. In itself alone the flesh is not life; it is of no avail on the supernatural plane, but when it is the flesh of the Word, it is life and gives life to others. From this principle he derived a series of fundamental conclusions:

1. Everything that takes place in Christ's humanity had a transcendent soteriological value that is now transmitted to us and in some way verified in us.[50]

2. What the Word of God worked visibly during his earthly life by means of his flesh, like miracles, etc., he now does invisibly, but really, by means of the Eucharist:

a) his flesh which was alive and life-giving now gives life to us;

b) what came about through the incarnation is now reproduced in us through participation in communion;

c) by receiving the life-giving flesh of the Lord, we receive the Spirit of Christ;

d) and are united: 1) to him; 2) with the Holy Spirit; 3) and therefore with the Father; 4) also among ourselves (the mystical body); and this is not only 5) psychologically (*kata schesin*) but also physically (*physikos, kata physin*); 6) even though it is a mystery how this comes about, it nevertheless comes about "bodily" (*somatikos, kata sarka*), whereby we become "concorporeal" (*syssomoi*) with Christ, and also "spiritually" (*pneumatikos, kata pneuma, en pneumati*) be-

---

50. "Everything that comes about in Christ comes about on account of us and for us and has the power of dispelling and destroying the evils that most justly have come to us as a result of our estrangement from God," **In Jo**. XII (PG 74, 628).

Cyril, especially, asserts the soteriological value of the various things that Christ did and suffered in his flesh: the incarnation, birth, baptism, miracles, passion, death, resurrection, ascension. See E. Meersch, **Le corps mystique du Christ** (Paris, 1936), pp. 494-97. The principle is: "Everything that comes about in Christ is for us." **Thesaurus** XX (PG 75, 333).

cause we receive the same Spirit of Christ; 7) in this process both our body and soul are implicated, and the divine life penetrates both.

The center of this whole process is Christ. "Indeed, the bond of unity is Christ, who at once is both God and man."[51]

In Christ himself the point of contact and exchange with us is more precisely his body as the Word's instrument.

The texts in which Cyril asserts this question are numerous. We shall record three of the most meaningful.

"Let they who have not accepted faith in Christ through stupidity hear: *if you do not eat the flesh of the Son of Man and drink his blood, you shall not have eternal life in you.* Those who do not receive Jesus in the mystical *Eulogia* will stay completely deprived and empty of the holy and blessed life. In fact, he is the eternal life by nature in that he is generated by the living Father. His holy body is no less life-giving since in some way it has been brought together and united with the Word in an ineffable manner. Therefore it is called his own and forms one person with him. After the incarnation Christ is inseparable, since, as we know, the Word that proceeds from the Father and the temple formed of the Virgin are not the same by nature. The body is not consubstantial with the Word of God. But they are one through an incomprehensible union and concurrence. And therefore since the flesh of the Savior has become life-giving since it is united to what is life by nature, the Word of God, when we experience it, we have life in us also, because we are united with this flesh as it is with the Word that dwells within it.

"By the same motive we see that when the Savior raised the dead he worked efficaciously not only by means of words and commands, as befitted God, but to this end he used principally also his holy flesh, to demonstrate that it could

---

51. **In Jo. Comm.** XI, 11 (PG 74, 560).

give life and was one with him. The body was truly his own
and not that of another. . . .

"Therefore, if what had been corrupted had been vivified
solely through contact with his holy flesh, how could we not
obtain this life-giving blessing more fully by tasting this flesh?
It will completely transform those who will participate in it,
and make them share in its own blessing which is immortality."[52]

" 'It is the Spirit that gives life, the flesh is of no avail.'
(John 6:63). He said: it is not without some good reason that
you have attributed to the flesh the incapacity to give life. If
we consider merely the nature of the flesh in itself, it is obvious that it is not life-giving. In no way can it give life to
anything; it needs one who can give it life. But when we consider diligently the mystery of the incarnation, and think about
who it is that dwells in this flesh, you will be completely disposed, if you do not wish to contradict the same Holy Spirit,
to admit that the flesh can give life, even though by itself it
is of no avail.

"From the moment that this flesh is united to the life-giving
Word, it has become completely life-giving, raised to the
power of a higher agent, without having violence done in
any way to its nature, and without the Word in any way being
humiliated. Therefore, although of itself the nature of the
flesh is incapable of giving life, once it has the life-giving
Word within it, it can give life since it has received all the force
of the Word. Indeed, it is the body of Life by its very nature
and not the body of some earthly man, about which it may
be rightly said that the flesh is of no avail. This is accomplished
in us by the flesh of no other man, like Paul or Peter, for example. The sole exception is the flesh of the Savior in whom
dwells 'the fullness of deity bodily' (Colossians 2:9). [53]

---

52. **ibid.**, IV, 2 (PG 73, 577).
53. **ibid.**, IV, 3 (PG 73, 601).

"Let us consider how we also, bodily and spiritually, are one with one another and with God. The Only-Begotten proceeds from the same substance of the Father and has the whole of the Father in his nature. When he became flesh, he blended, as it were, with our nature through an ineffable union with an earthly body. Thus, this true God has become really a heavenly man, not a man who merely 'bears' God, as those who do not comprehend precisely the depth of the mystery say. He is at the same time God and man, unites in some way in himself what is most different by nature, and makes man a consort and a sharer of the divine nature.

"Participation in the Holy Spirit is communicated to him; the Spirit has also dwelt in us. This has begun in Christ and is first verified in him. For, when he became like us, a man, he was anointed and consecrated, in his divine nature, as well, and insofar as he proceeds from the Father, he himself sanctifies by the Spirit this very temple and the whole universe created by him, and he also must be sanctified.

"The mystery of Christ is therefore the beginning and the way whereby we have become sharers of the Spirit, and united with God. All are sanctified with him in this manner.

"But since we too were united and fused, as it were, with God and with one another, although we are with our soul and body separate and distinct persons, the Only-Begotten has devised a means worthy of his wisdom and of the Father's counsel.

"In one body, his own, he blesses (and transforms) in mystic communion the faithful who believe in him, and makes them 'con-corporeal' with him and among themselves.

"Who can divide them? Who could deprive them of their physical union, when they are bound together in unity with Christ by means of his holy body? . . . Since we are all united with one and the same Christ through his holy body, and we all receive in our bodies the one and indivisible Christ, we must look upon our own members as belonging more to him than to ourselves. . . .

4 The Flesh

"St. Paul attests to the fact that we who partake of his holy flesh have also a bodily union with Christ . . . (Ephesians 3:5 ff.). If we are all of one body with one another and also with him, this is manifestly because he is in us with his own flesh. How will we not clearly be one, both among ourselves and with Christ? Indeed, Christ is the bond of unity, being at the same time God and man.

"As for the union in the Spirit, we shall say, following the same mode of thought, that in receiving this same and unique Spirit, we are all fused with one another and with God. . . . For, just as the power of the holy flesh makes those receiving it 'con-corporeal,' it is in the same way, I think, that the one and indivisible Spirit of God, dwelling in us, makes us all into a spiritual union. . . . Since a unique Spirit dwells in us the one God will also be in us, the Father of all who through the Son makes us one with himself and with all who participate in his Spirit. . . . Thus we are all one with the Father, the Son and the Holy Spirit; we are one by identity of condition — let us remember what was said in the beginning — and in the conformity of piety, and in the communion in the holy flesh of Christ, and in the fellowship of the one Spirit, as we have said."[54]

---

54. **Ibid.**, XI, 11 (PG 74, 557-561).

VI

BODY OF CHRIST, SALVATION AND EUCHARIST, ACCORDING TO ST. THOMAS

For our subject, St. Thomas' tracts on Christ, the sacraments, and especially the Eucharist, have special importance.

The formulation of these tracts naturally follows the general lines of the saintly Doctor's theology. As we know, it is concerned above all with the solution of questions of an ontological and almost metaphysical type, bearing on revelation; this is the primary aim, which he achieves through the instrumentality of philosophy and Aristotelian dialectics.

But it is also quite known that specifically on questions of Christology (and the sacraments) St. Thomas makes use of a great part of patristic tradition, including the Greek,[1] and seeks to integrate its most profound intuitions within the framework of his thought.

Therefore, when we bring together the sporadic statements he makes on the matter of our concern, we find that he has

---

1. See I. Backes, **Die Christologie des hl. Thomas von Aquin und die griechischen Väter** (Paderborn, 1931).

given us a markedly clear synthesis in the best lines of Scripture and tradition, together with additional valuable specifications that are the successful product of his most accurate metaphysical analyses of the matter being considered.

Three points deserve our attention: the body of Christ in St. Thomas' soteriology, his teaching on the contact we have with Christ's humanity through faith and the sacraments of faith, and his teaching on the Eucharist.

1) *The body of Christ in St. Thomas' soteriology*

St. Thomas is well aware of the teaching of the Greek Fathers on Christ's integral humanity, body and soul, as the Word's instrument in the salvation of the human race and in the continual application of this salvation to individuals who submit to him;[2] whereby Christ's integral humanity is vivified and gives life, sanctified and sanctifying.[3]

Although in his *Commentary on the Sentences* of Peter Lombard, St. Thomas is still remarkably hesitant, in the *Summa* he definitively probes deeper into this doctrine on two points. Above all, he gives us a very sharp metaphysical analysis of the notion of instrument and the *modus agendi* of the instrumental cause under the influence of the principal cause. In this action the instrument is transitorily raised to the *modus agendi* of the principal cause that makes use of it. Therefore, the total effect is able greatly to transcend what the instrumental cause could do by itself. This effect, furthermore, belongs completely both to the principal cause and the instrumental cause, although in a different way.

---

2. For example: **Summa III** 7 a 1 ad 3; 8 a 1 ad 1; 13 a 2 c.; 43 a 2 c.; 48 a 6 c.

3. **Summa III** 34 a 1 ad 3; 79 a 1 c. with the quotation from the text of St. Cyril of Alexandria, **In Lc. 22, 19** (PG 72, 92); **In. Jo. cap. VI, Lect. 6**, Marietti ed., p. 206.

In this context, St. Thomas adds the distinction between a living and conjoined instrument and a dead and separate one. In relation to the Word, Christ's human nature is an alive, conjoined and free instrument; on the other hand, the sacraments are instruments that are separate from the Word and from Christ's human nature.[4]

By means of the human soul the Word assumed the human body in the unity of his person and made use of it in Christ's life as a living and conjoined instrument in order to bring about the salvation of men.[5]

Secondly, St. Thomas distinguishes three sorts of grace in Christ: the grace of the hypostatic union; the personal grace of a single man, and the grace of the head of mankind or of the mystical body, the *gratia capitis*.

a) Christ's physical body and the *gratia capitis*.

The *gratia capitis* is essentially the same grace that Christ had as a single man, although it exists to such an eminent degree that it can flow over to others.[6] Therefore Christ is the Head, and exercises the function of Head, since in relation to others he is closer to the supreme font of grace, God himself, because he possesses the total fullness of grace, and finally because he communicates to them the grace he possesses.[7]

In this "capital" function, moreover, we are always dealing with Christ's integral human nature, body and soul, and he influences this divine life both in the bodies and souls of men, in particular ways. Therefore the man Christ, soul and body, is Head both of bodies and souls. Here is what St. Thomas

---

4. **Summa** III 7 a 1 ad 3; 13 a 2 c.; 62 a 5 c. On St. Thomas' position on this point in his **Commentary on the Sentences**, see R. Biagi, **La causalità dell'umanità di Cristo e dei sacramenti** (Bologna, 1965).

5. **Summa** III 6 a 1.

6. **Summa** III 8 a 5 and ad 3.

7. **Summa** III 8 a 1.

says precisely: "Christ's whole humanity, both body and soul, influences both the souls and the bodies of men. Principally in the soul, however, and secondarily in the bodies. In one way, insofar as the members of the body are subjected to the work of righteousness in the soul that lives for Christ, as the Apostle says (Romans 6:13). And in a second way insofar as the glorious life of the soul overflows in the body."[8]

And it is worthy of note that St. Thomas admits that since Christ, soul and body, can be the Head both of our souls and bodies, it is necessary that there be a certain continuity between Christ's physical body and our body: "our bodies in a certain way have a continuity with Christ's body; not quantitatively, nor in accordance with natural perfection, but insofar as the Holy Spirit dwells within us, who, himself was in Christ in fullness, as we read in the Epistle to the Corinthians (6:19): 'Do you not know that your members are temples of the Holy Spirit?' "[9]

The answer is even more fitting if we add to it, as St. Thomas does in the doctrine on the Eucharist, the very special nature of the contact between Christ's physical body and our body in the Eucharist. This shows once again that it is precisely corporeity that is the point of contact between Christ and us.

All of this is valid not only for men after the incarnation but in a certain sense also for those who came before. For even they did not attain salvation except through their faith in the Christ who was to come. Even then, through the faith of the believers, Christ's humanity, which in some way they reached and touched as already existing in the intentions and eternal designs of God, had an influence on the justification of men.[10]

St. Thomas is of the opinion that Christ as man, including his body, is the Head also of the angels and his humanity in-

---

8. **Summa** III 8 a 2 c. See 4 ad 1; 3 d 13 q 2 a 2 q 3.

9. 3 d 13 q 2 a 2 q 3 ad 1.

10. **Summa** III 6 a 3 ad 3; 68 a 1 ad 1; **De Verit.** 29 a 5 ad 9.

cluding the physical body, as an instrument of the divinity, also influences them. Christ as man is Head both of men and of angels "because he is closer to God and possesses his gifts more perfectly not only than men but also than the angels; and because it is not only men who receive his influence but also the angels. In fact, we read (Ephesians 1:20) that God the Father set Christ 'at his right hand in the heavenly places, far above all rule and authority and power and dominion, and above every name that is named, not only in this age but also in that which is to come; and he has put all things under his feet.' Therefore Christ is Head not only of men but also of the angels. Thus in Matthew (4:11) we read: 'and behold, angels came and ministered to him.' "[11] In another place, St. Thomas tells us: "The humanity of Christ, by the power of his spiritual nature, i.e. the divine nature, can be the cause of something not only in the spirits of men but also in the spirits of angels because of its supreme conjoinedness with God, i.e. the personal union."[12]

St. Thomas further observes that "although the corporeal nature is inferior to the nature of the spirit, the nature of Christ's body transcends every spirit, since it is united to the divinity; this union is greater and more worthy than the union that comes about through the enjoyment of God."[13]

Here, if I am not mistaken, are the ultimate consequences of the doctrine of man's corporeity in the Bible, and of the basic statement of Christian faith that the Word assumed an integral human nature, body and soul, in the incarnation: Christ as man, including his body, is the Head of every creature.

It is undeniable that similar notions are perfectly framed

---

11. **Summa** III 8 a 4 c.

12.**Ibid.**, ad 3. See also **De Verit**. 29 a 5c. In referring to a thought of Dionysius, St. Thomas says that Christ as man "illumines the angels" (**De Verit**. 29 a 4 c.; 3 d 13 q 2 a 2 q 1.).

13. 3 d 22 q 3 a 3 q 1 ad 3.

in St. Paul's view expressed in the Epistle to the Colossians (1:15-20), and in the text from Ephesians which St. Thomas so successfully uses here. What he points out is most valuable and shows, I think, the way that needs to be followed for a deep understanding of the relations between Christ as man and the angels. I do not see why, within the logic of St. Paul's statements in Colossians and Ephesians, and St. Thomas' observations, it is not necessary to say that the grace of the angels also comes from Christ the Mediator. If the angels were put to the test, then we must admit that it was a test of faith. In that case there is nothing to prevent us from saying that the object of this test was the future incarnation and that, within the historical plan of the divine economy in regard to creatures, every grace given by God to a being, was and still is given by him in virtue of the future or past merits of the humanity of the Incarnate Word. The force of Scripture and tradition converge in this unitary perspective, centered on Christ, of God's whole work directed towards his creatures.

St. Thomas is easily able to arrive at this point, after his accurate metaphysical analysis of the notion of instrumental causality, its *modus agendi* and its efficaciousness under the influence of the principal cause; in its action the instrumental cause is raised to the dignity of this principal cause.

b) The causality exercised in our salvation by what Christ did and suffered in his mortal flesh.

In this same persepective St. Thomas goes back to the statements of the Greek Fathers: that all that Christ did and suffered in his flesh had and has salvific value for men. "We must assert that what Christ suffered or did in his human nature, freeing us from both spiritual and bodily ills, has brought us spiritual and eternal goods."[14]

---

14. **Compend. theol.** chap. 241, n. 520.

Its ultimate reason is this: "all that Christ did or suffered were instrumental actions of the divine power directed toward the salvation of men."[15]

For St. Thomas, furthermore, everything that Christ did and suffered in his flesh still has causal influence on the salvation of every man, and did not merely have that influence in the past. How is this possible since these events were limited to space and time? St. Thomas answers that in these events the divine power operated through its instrument: "this divine power personally reaches all places and all times. And this contact of power is sufficient to explain their efficaciousness"[16] which reaches all men at all times and in all places.

What is this causal influence? Here again St. Thomas can give us valuable specifications through the analysis to which he subjected the notion of a cause and the various types of causality.

He explains that this influence always includes an efficient instrumental causality, as well as an exemplary causality, but not always a meritorious causality. A causality that is also meritorious existed only in what Christ did and suffered in his mortal flesh, from the first moment of the incarnation to the last instant of his life upon the cross. In what happened afterward, Christ did not merit.

What does he mean by a non-meritorious efficient causality in the grace given to men by his descent into the lower regions, his resurrection and ascension? He means an influence that is always an instrument of the divine power in the production of this grace, insofar as it is also a created reality from a certain point of view.[17] He means also an influence in the application or distribution of this grace to individuals.

---

15. **Summa** III 48 a 6 c.

16. **Summa** III 56 a 1 ad 3.

17. We must understand this well in order not to slip into unacceptable materializations of grace. There is the whole question of this created grace which certainly responds to a reality, one that is mysterious but

The exemplary causality of the birth of our Lord means, for example, that Christ, born among men, obtains for us and gives us the right to be born to new life; that of death, a dying to the old man, and of resurrection, a rising to a new life in God, etc.

Thus St. Thomas, in that part of his tract on Christ in which he explains the various occurrences in the life .of the Savior, from his conception to the ascension, does not neglect to point out the salvific value of each of these in its time and in its place.[18]

He obviously dwells in a special way on the passion, death, descent into the lower regions, resurrection and ascension: the central events of the paschal mystery in Christ.

St. Thomas accurately distinguishes the various aspects of the causality of the passion of Christ in our salvation, always as an instrument of the divinity: its efficient, meritorious, satisfactory, redemptive, sacrificial, and (as he points out specifically) also its exemplary causality.[19]

He specifies the respective roles played by the soul and the body in the merit of the passion: "the principle of the merit is in the soul; the body is the instrument of the meritorious act."[20]

All that Christ did and suffered in his flesh from the first moment of his conception, had, as an instrument of the divinity, the potency of merit and satifaction, sufficient for the redemption of the world;[21] but the passion was necessary on the pre-

---

undeniable since grace is also something which really transforms man into a new creature and cannot be simply a non-imputation of guilt.

18. **Summa** III 31-58. Note specially: incarnation, III 31 a 1 c.; circumcision, 37 a 1 ad 3; observance of the prescriptions of the law, 37 a 3 c.; poverty: 40 a 3 c.; the temptation in the desert, 41 a I; the miracles, see for example 44 a 3; the transfiguration, 45 a 1 and a 4 ad 2.

19. **Summa** III 48 al − a 6; 49 a 1, and for example, **ibid.**, **49** a 3 ad 3.

20. **Summa** III 49 a 6 ad 1.

21. **Summa** III 34 a 3; 3 d 18 a 5.

supposition that God had in fact willed that only in the case where this meritorious cause reached all the preceding ones, would our liberation and the exaltation of Christ come about. "Nothing prevents one thing from depending on different causes. Thus Christ was able to merit through later acts and sufferings that glory of immortality that he merited at the first instant of his conception, although not yet in the sense that it was so much his due, but that it was owed him through various causes."[22]

Thus, without excluding the meritorious causality of the other events in the life of the Lord, in the historical order effectively willed by God, Christ's passion appears still as the meritorious and determining satisfactory cause of our redemption, and the whole life of the Lord seems pervaded by the tension of his passion. Therefore, the means of salvation, the sacraments instituted by Christ, derive their efficaciousness from the Savior's passion.[23]

All of this is always in virtue of the principle that Christ's body was the instrument of the divinity which operated through it.

He also analyzes the causality of Christ's death in relation to our salvation. The moments that preceded the separation of his body and soul are still the passion and they have the same soteriological value as the passion. At the moment that the separation took place between his body and soul, Christ's merit ceased. But this does not mean that every efficient and exemplary causal influence of his body on our salvation also ceased. "The divinity, therefore, was not separated from Christ's flesh even by death. Thus, everything that happened in Christ's flesh, even after the soul was separated from it, was salutary for us because of the divine power that was

---

22. **Summa III 46 a 1; a 2 and ad 1; 34 a 3 ad 3; see also ibid., 48 a 1 ad 2 and ad 3; 59 a 3 c.; Suppl. 76 a 1 ad 2.
23. **Summa III 49 a 1 ad 4; 62 a 5.   6

united to it. . . . Through Christ's death, we are told, the death of the soul caused by our sin was destroyed — as we see from the Epistle to the Romans, 4:25: Christ was put to death for our trespasses — and the death of the body, which consists in the separation from the soul, was also destroyed, as we are told in the Epistle to the Corinthians 15:54: 'Death is swallowed up in victory.' "[24]

Something similar also took place in the burial of the Lord.[25]

c) The causality exercised upon our salvation by the resurrection and the ascension of the Lord and by his flesh in glory.

His causality exercises even greater influence on our own salvation, as was and is verified in his glorious flesh.

Although in his explanation of the "necessity of the resurrection" St. Thomas makes use of *rationes convenientiae* (congruent or fitting reasons),[26] he is nevertheless quite well aware that we can speak of necessity on the historical level, when we consider the effective manner in which God freely in his wisdom willed that our salvation be realized in the past and at present.[27] On this level, he is able to say that the incarnation or the other works done or suffered by Christ during his life for our salvation were not "a proximate, but rather a remote disposition of our resurrection of body and soul."[28]

As for the type of causality through which the resurrection of Christ influences us, we must say that it is both an efficient

---

24. Summa III 50 a 6c.

25. Summa III 51 a 1 and ad 1, a 2 ad 4.

26. Summa III 53 a 1.

27. Summa III 56 a 1 ad 2; 46 a 2; Suppl. 76 a 1 ad 2.

28. 3 d 21 q 2 a 1 ad 2. "The proximate disposition to our resurrection is not the Word made flesh, but the Word made flesh and rising from the dead." See also Summa, Suppl. 76 a 1 ad 2 and ad 3.

instrumental cause and an exemplary cause of our resurrection of body and soul.

In this way we can better understand the relations between the passion, death and resurrection of Christ under this particular aspect: "in the justification of souls two things concur: the remission of guilt and the newness of life through grace. Therefore, both the passion of Christ and his resurrection are the cause of both things, in the area of efficaciousness brought about by the divine power. As for the exemplary causality, properly speaking, Christ's passion and death are the cause of the remission of guilt whereby we die to sin; while the resurrection of Christ is the cause of the new life that comes from grace or righteousness. Therefore the Apostle says in Romans 4:25: 'he was put to death for our trespasses'; and so that they might be taken away 'he was raised for our justification.' But the passion of Christ is also a meritorious cause."[29]

In the resurrection of Christ his body and not only his soul influences both our bodies and our souls, although as an instrument of the divinity.[30]

Christ's resurrection will be the instrumental cause of our future resurrection.[31]

The ascension of Christ is also a cause of our salvation. Although it is not yet a meritorious cause, it is an efficient, instrumental and exemplary cause, since "it is the cause of our ascension, insofar as it gives a beginning to it in our Head to whom the members will have to be conformed."[32] In ascending into heaven, Christ prepares the way for us do likewise, beseeches the Father that we might follow him, and gives us the gifts that will enable us to do so in fact.[33]

According to St. Thomas' principles, we ought not to think

---

29. Summa III 56 a 2 ad 4. See also a 1 ad 3 snd ad 4; **Suppl.** 76 a 1.
30. Summa III 57 a 2 ad 2; **Compend. Theol.**, cap. 239.
31. **Summa, Suppl.** 76 a 1 and ad 3.
32. **Summa** III, 57 a 6 ad 2.
33. **Summa** III 57 a 6c

that the soteriological function of the Lord's body reaches its term for us in this life and not with our future resurrection. It always exercises its mediatory, efficient and exemplary function even in heaven with the blessed and above all in the grace of the beatific vision that they enjoy and which is the goal of the whole economy of salvation. And if we logically follow through the thought of St. Paul (Ephesians 1:20-23; Colossians 1:15-20; 2:10) and of St. Thomas himself, this is equally true in regard to the angels.

Furthermore, St. Thomas expressly points out that the blessed, after their resurrection, will also see bodily in the glorious body of Christ the reflection and the more wonderful transparent concretization of God himself and his glory: in a sense similar to when we see a man moving, speaking, etc., and say that we do not only believe in life or understand it but also *see* it. He is speaking here, basically, of a global psychological intuition in which even the senses have their noteworthy role. Nature's poetic and especially mystical intuition in relation to God can give us at least a vague idea of this. Here is what St. Thomas says: "Since the eyes and the senses will be in the glorious body in the same way that they are at present, they will not be able to see the divine essence as something seen, since it is in itself invisible. But they will see it as something which is visible *per accidens*. In fact, the eyes of the body will see so much glory in the bodies, chiefly in the glorious bodies and most especially in the body of Christ, and furthermore the intellect will see God so clearly, that man will perceive God in the things that he sees bodily just as life is perceived in speech. Although our intellect will not see God by means of creatures, still it will see him in the creature that it sees bodily. In *De civitate Dei* (22:29), Augustine explains the manner in which God will be able to be seen bodily in this way: 'we must believe that then we shall see created things, the new heaven and the new earth, in such a way that with the greatest clarity we shall see ... God above all, as present in and governing created things. Not as we do now when we see the invisible perfections of God by means of created things, but as when we even barely see men; we do not *believe* that they live, but we *see* them."[34]

Throughout all eternity the vision of the glorious body of Christ will constitute the chief object of what is called our *accidental* beatitude.

In conclusion, St. Thomas supplies us with some noteworthy contributions toward a deeper understanding of the question of the soteriological function of Christ's body on the bases of what the Greek Fathers had said about its salvific importance in the incarnation and all that Christ did and suffered in his flesh. This contribution is possible for him for three chief seasions: 1. through a deeper analysis of the notion of instrument and of its elevation under the influence of the principal cause, insofar as the dignity and power of the effect is measured in the light of the principal cause and not the mere instrumental cause; 2. through the notion of the *gratia capitis;* and 3. through a better distinction between efficient cause and meritorious and exemplary cause.

2) *Faith and the sacraments as the indispensable means of salutary contact with the life-giving flesh of Christ and with what he did and suffered in the flesh*

Therefore, for St. Thomas, as for the New Testament and the tradition of the Fathers, Christ's flesh and what he did and suffered in his flesh within God's effectively willed economy, is of essential, and henceforth eternal, importance in the process whereby men attain their supernatural goal.

The entire Christian life is nothing else than a participation

---

34. **Summa, Suppl.** 92 a 1 c.

by individuals in the divine realities that came to pass in Christ, in his flesh, a participation which has its effect in configuring men to the model himself.

With the Fathers, St. Thomas repeats that in everything done and suffered by the Word in his flesh mankind was included in the sense that whatever took place in the Head, can and even by right must be fulfilled in each individual. Through the incarnation all human nature can and must be assumed and divinized by the Word through its participation in and imitation of Christ. Through Jesus' birth, every man can and must be born in divine life; through his death each man can and must die to the old man, etc. All of this is the result of the fact that God constituted Christ as our Head, and therefore everything that was given to Christ was also given to us in Christ. "Since Christ is our Head, what was given to Christ was given also to us in him. Because of this, since he has already risen, the Apostle tells us that in a certain way God has raised us with him, even though we ourselves are not yet risen, but shall be, as the Epistle to the Romans (8:11) says: 'he who raised Christ Jesus from the dead will give life to your mortal bodies.' In line with the same thought, the Apostle adds: 'he has made us to sit along with him in the heavens,' i.e. by the fact that Christ our Head is already there. . . ."[35] In another place St. Thomas states: "Through his passion, Christ has freed us from sin by instituting the cause, i.e. the cause of our liberation, whereby whatever sin committed at whatever moment of the past, present or future, can be forgiven; as if a physician had made a medicine that cured every possible malady, even in the future."[36]

But since this happens not merely by right but also *de facto* and actually in each individual, it is necessary that the expiatory, efficient and exemplary salvific power of what Christ

---

35. **Summa** III 58 a 4 ad 1.
36. Summa III 49 a 1 ad 3.

did and suffered in his flesh be applied to everyone, and that everyone thereby enter in some way into contact with this same power.

This contact of salvation, as St. Thomas tirelessly repeats,[37] is a unique reality that by the wisdom of God's positive will has at once two aspects: one is the spiritual, because it must come about with our spirit, and the other bodily, because our bodies must also enter into it. The concrete man who must be saved is a unity of spirit and body; and Christ, with whom we must enter into contact in order to receive salvation, is both spirit and body. Therefore, also our contact with what he did and suffered in his flesh must be made in the soul, which is realized in faith (hope and charity), *and* in the body which is accomplished through the sacraments of the faith: rites that are also sensory and external in which the body is also involved.

"With regard to grace, the sacraments operate as instruments. St. John Damascene (*De Fide Orthodoxa*, bk. III, ch. XIII) says that Christ's human nature was the instrument of divinity. Thus his human nature participated to some extent in what the divine power did. For example, Christ healed the leper in touching him, which meant that in an instrumental way contact with Christ caused the leper's return to health. Since Christ's human nature was the instrument for realizing the effects of the divine power in corporeal things, the same is true for the spiritual. Therefore Christ's blood shed for us has the power of washing away our sins. He washed us of our sins in his blood, says Revelation (1:5); we are justified in his blood, says the Epistle to the Romans (3:24). Thus Christ's humanity is the instrumental cause of our justification. *This cause is applied to us spiritually by means of faith, and corporeally by means of the sacraments, because Christ's humanity*

---

37. For example: **De Veritate** 27 a 4 c.; **Summa** III 48 a 6 ad 2; 49 tionem unitatem accepterunt. **ibid.** III 17, 2.
a 6 c.; 4 d 1 q 2 a 6 q 2 ad 3; **Contra Gent.** IV 56.

is both spirit and body,"[38] and also, as St. Thomas explains elsewhere at length,[39] because man is spirit and body.

In the mind of St. Thomas this faith which in the sacraments applies to every man the salutary power of what Christ did and suffered in his flesh, is not some ordinary kind of faith but faith formed in charity.[40]

Furthermore, St. Thomas' thought is that faith and the sacraments are not two juxtaposed and parallel ways for achieving the same goal with faith on one side and the sacraments on the other, but rather one unique way, one reality: faith professed and embodied in the sacramental rite, which is at the same time a profession of faith and certified by charity.

Therefore the sacraments' efficacity "comes from three things: the divine institution as the principal cause, the passion of Christ as the meritorious cause, and the faith of the Church as that which places the instrument in continuity with the principal agent."[41]

In the context immediately preceding this statement, St. Thomas has this to say: "The instrument does not have power in the aforesaid manner except insofar as it is in continuity with the principal agent, in order that the power of this agent be transfused into the instrument. The principal cause of justification is God as the efficient cause, the passion of Christ as the meritorious cause. The Sacrament is in continuity with this cause through the faith of the Church which refers the in-

---

39. **Summa** III 61 a 1 and ad 1 and ad 2.; **C. Gent.** IV 56.

38. **De Verit.** 27 a 4 c.

40. The principal is general: the faith that saves us is that faith that is formed in charity: **Summa III** 49 a 15. For the sacraments St. Thomas at different times instead of using the expression "what saves is the faith and the sacraments," will say that what saves is "faith and charity and the sacraments of the faith." **Ibid.**, III 49 a 3 ad 1; a 5 c.

41. 4 d 1 q 1 a 4 q 3.

strument to the principal agent and the sign to the thing signifying."[42]

In continuing a patristic tradition,[43] St. Thomas observes that the sacramental rites themselves have a corporeo-spiritual and human-divine structure, similar to the Word Incarnate himself, whose separate instruments they are, just as his human nature including his body is his conjoined and living instrument.

Indeed, the sacraments are a reality composed of a sensory element, e.g., water, bread, wine, acts of the penitent, and a spiritual and spiritualizing element, the word that determines the significance of the foregoing sensory element and is the object of faith. And all of this, says St. Thomas, harmonizes very well with the same corporeo-spiritual structure of human nature.

The sacraments may first be considered "from the viewpoint of the sanctifying cause who is the Incarnate Word. In a certain way, the sacrament has the same structure insofar as in it the word is added to a sensory thing, just as in the mystery of the incarnation the Word of God is united to the sensory flesh.

"Secondly, we may look upon the sacraments from the point of view of the man who is sanctified; he is composed of body and soul. The 'remedy' of the sacrament is proportioned to him, and it reaches the body through a sensory thing, and in the word used in it the 'remedy' is the object of faith."[44]

---

42. See also **Summa** III 49 a 6 ad 2: "Although the passion of Christ is corporeal it nevertheless has a spiritual efficacity by virtue of the united deity. And it therefore obtains efficacity by spiritual contact, i.e., through the faith and the sacraments of the faith." **Summa** III 61 a 1 ad 1: "in the use of the sacraments the action of the body is not purely corporeal, but in some way spiritual, viz. through what it signifies and what it causes." "The sacraments are signs that manifest the faith whereby man is justified." **Summa** III 62 a 4 c.

43. See E. H. Schillebeeckx, **De sacramentelle heilseconomie** (Antwerp, 1952), pp. 355-364.

44. **Summa** III 60 a 6c.

In the *Contra Gentiles* (IV 56), we have some excellent formulas which illustrate the following motives that explain God's wisdom in giving an incarnate form even to the means of salvation: "especially because God provided for man, as for other things, in accordance with what his nature required. Man's nature is to be led to an understanding of spiritual things through sensory things. The sacraments of the Church are precisely of this type. It was therefore necessary to give these remedies of salvation through sensory things. Secondly this was done because it is necessary that the instrument be proportioned to the first cause. The first and universal cause of human salvation is the Incarnate Word, as is evident from what we have said above. It was therefore fitting that these remedies, whereby the power of the universal cause could reach men, have a likeness to that cause insofar as in them the divine power works invisibly under sensory signs.... From this must be excluded the error of some heretics who would wish that all these visible things be excluded from the sacraments of the Church. This is nothing extraordinary, for they are of the opinion that all visible things, by nature, are evil and were produced by an evil cause.

"... And it is not unfitting that spiritual salvation be given through visible and bodily things, since these visible things are instruments, as it were, of the Incarnate God who underwent the passion. The instrument does not operate by virtue of its own nature, but in virtue of the principal agent through which it has been applied to the action."

We can now see the extent of the importance of the sarcicopneumatic structure of the whole economy of salvation. The spirit dwells in the body and compenetrates it; the *pneuma* inhabits the *sarx* and divinizes it, and through the instrument of the body and the sensory, the suprasensory and the divine are communicated.

For St. Thomas this word pair *faith-sacrament* is so characteristic of God's willed plan of salvation for mankind that after Adam's sin it is valid also for men before the coming of

Christ. What saved them was the faith in the coming Christ, professed and embodied in certain rites that for them had the value of sacraments and placed them in contact with the Incarnate Word, specifically with his passion, insofar as it already existed in the mind of God.[45]

However, at least for baptism and penance — and as we shall see further on, for the Eucharist — St. Thomas knew the distinction between the use of the sacraments *in re* and *in voto*. "The sacrament works in two ways: the first is presented in the act, and the second in the desire. This is verified because the sacraments work as instruments of God's mercy justifying men. But God sees the hearts of men, as we read in 1 Samuel 16:7: 'man looks on the outward appearance, but the Lord looks on the heart.' Therefore, although material things act only if they are used, the sacraments still act even when they are only desired. But they more fully produce their effect when they are presented in act, as baptism."[46]

This is one of the elements where in St. Thomas' way of treating the sacraments we see the pre-eminence of the aspect of faith (hope, charity) over the aspect of the bare rite, as well as the indispensibility of the rite itself.

St. Thomas naturally does not forget that for salvation man must be conformed to Christ, specifically to the suffering Christ, in his whole moral life.

This is precisely because what saves is not the mere sacraments without faith, hope and charity, nor mere faith without reference to the sacraments, but faith embodied in the sacraments: our conformation to what Christ did and suffered in his flesh is dynamic and successive. In fact, faith hope and charity must always grow in order to give life to the sacrament and be themselves further vivified.[47]

---

45. **Summa** III 61 a 3 c.; 62 a 6 c.
46. **Quodl.** 4 q 7 a 10 c. See also ad 2 and ad 3.
47. **Summa** III 49 a 3 ad 3; a 4 c. in fine; 56 a 1 ad 1.

3) *Corporeity and Eucharist in St. Thomas*

With St. Thomas, the doctrine of corporeity in the general plan of salvation culminates, within the thought lines of the New Testament and the Greek Fathers, with the doctrine of the Eucharist.

a) In general

A synthetic statement of his view on corporeity-Eucharist is to be found in the text of the *De Veritate* which we have cited in part above, and which we shall now have to broach in its entirety.

Here he treats the question of whether or not the sacraments of the new law are a cause of grace, and if they are in what particular manner is this true of them. Here is what St. Thomas replies: "Neither a sacrament nor any other creature can give grace as one who has grace of himself, since this prerogative belongs solely to the divine power, as is clear from what we have said in the preceding article. The sacraments operate as instruments in regard to grace; which is explained in the following way.

"St. John Damascene (*De Fide Orthodoxa,* bk. III, ch. XIII) says that Christ's human nature was the instrument of the divinity. His human nature therefore participated in what the divine nature did. For example, Christ healed the leper by touching him; contact with Christ instrumentally caused the healing of the leper. Since Christ's human nature was the instrument bringing about the effects of the divine power in bodily things, the same is true for the spiritual. Therefore Christ's blood shed for us had the power of washing away our sins. He washed us of our sins in his blood, says Revelation (1:5); we are justified in his blood, the Epistle to the Romans tells us (3:24). Thus Christ's humanity is the instrumental cause of our justification.

"This cause is applied to us spiritually by means of faith,

and corporeally by means of the sacraments, because Christ's humanity is both spirit and body, with the purpose of our receiving that sanctification that comes from Christ.

"*Therefore* the most perfect sacrament is that in which Christ's body is really contained, the Eucharist, which brings to perfection the act of all the other sacraments, as Dionysius says (*Eccl. Hier.* III).

"On the other hand, the other sacraments share only some part of that power whereby the humanity of Christ instrumentally works out our justification. Therefore the Apostle says (Romans 5:9) that whoever is sanctified in baptism is sanctified in the blood of Christ."[48]

Here is a general summary of his reasoning: Christ was spirit and body. His humanity, including his body, was and is the instrument of the divinity in working out man's salvation. In order to be saved, we must enter into bodily and spiritual contact with this humanity, including Christ's body. This comes about through faith and in the sacraments. *Therefore*, the most perfect sacrament is the one in which Christ's body is contained in a real way. The other sacraments only participate in part of the instrumental salvific power of Christ's humanity.

In the *Commentaries on the Sentences of Peter Lombard* we find further specifications. Why only in this union with Christ, which includes also a union with his body, do we find the greatest perfection of the Christian?

St. Thomas explains it by referring to the general metaphysical principal that the greatest perfection of a thing in the supreme development of its own form of being and acting is found only in its being conjoined with the ultimate principal from which its own being is derived.[49]

In Christian life the ultimate principal from which everything derives (and St. Thomas understands here the ultimate

---

48. **De Verit.** 27 a 4 c.

49. **Anathema** 11 (approved with the rest at the council of Ephesus)

instrumental and integral principal) is the humanity of Christ, including his body.

Therefore, he concludes, only in the union that includes Christ's body do we have the greatest perfection of the Christian: that which happens in the Eucharist, which precisely for this reason is the "perfection of perfections."[50]

But why precisely in the Eucharist is our greatest union with Christ, including his body, verified? Because not only is Christ's body really present there, but the union that takes place is so intimate that it is proposed to us under the sensory figure of assimilation in the manner of food. This, however, does not so much mean our profound assimilation of Christ as it does the fact of Christ's conjoining and profoundly assimilating us to himself by transforming us in himself. "Fittingly," says St. Thomas, "this sacrament was instituted under the figure of food. Among the other senses it is the tactile sense that is really conjoined with its object. . . . Taste is a kind of touch. And among the other things that pertain to the sense of touch, only in eating is there produced the conjunction between the food and what is eaten, because the food and the one nourished by it become one. . . . Therefore, although every sacrament must be proposed under the figure of something sensory, it is fitting that under the figure of food we have presented to us this sacrament in which the Incarnate Word is contained for the purpose of being united with us. This comes about not because he becomes changed into us by being conjoined with us, but rather because he changes us into himself by means of his being joined with us. Augustine (*Confessions,* VII 10) puts these words into the mouth of the Incarnate Word: 'Thou shout not change me into thyself as food of thy flesh; but thou shalt be changed in me.' "[51]

Here then we have the answer: "For our perfection it was

---

50. **Ibid.**, ad 2.
51. 4 d 8 q 1 a 3 q 1.

necessary for our Head to be conjoined with us in a real manner."[52]

b) Sacrament of the passion or also of the resurrection?

Along with the New Testament and the whole of tradition, St. Thomas insists upon the special relationship of the Eucharist with the passion of Christ. "The Eucharist is the perfect sacrament of the Lord's passion since it contains the same Christ who suffered — *ipsum Christum passum*";[53] it is the "sacrament of the passion of Christ, since man is perfected in the union with the Christ who suffered — *ad Christum passum.*"[54] Through the separation of the species of bread and wine, we have a representation of Christ's passion "in which the blood was separated from the body."[55]

Therefore the Eucharist can especially be called "the sacrament of the Lord's passion, containing the *Christum passum* in itself. And consequently, everything that is the effect of the Lord's passion is also the effect of this sacrament. In fact, this sacrament is nothing else than the application of the Lord's passion to us."[56]

But St. Thomas does not wish to exclude a real relationship of the Eucharist with the resurrection and the risen Christ.

As a matter of fact, in this same commentary on John's Gospel that we have just cited, after having said that everything that is the effect of the passion is also the effect of the Eucharist, he continues: "it is clear therefore that the destruction of death wrought by Christ in dying, and the reparation of life accomplished by Christ in rising from the dead, are the

---

52. **Ibid.,** q 1 a 1 q a 3.
53. **Summa** III 73 a 5 ad 2.
54. **Summa** III 73 a 3 ad 3.
55. **Summa** III 76 a 2 ad 1. See 74 a 1 c.
56. **In Jo. cap. VI, lect. VI** to the end. See also **Summa** III 4 a 1 c.; 79 a 1 c.

effect of this sacrament,"[57] which implies that the Eucharist in some way is also the sacrament of resurrection. From the very beginning the liturgies have made this clear by suitably extending the notion of the *anamnesis* in the Eucharist to include the resurrection.

St. Thomas does not clarify this point. We must acknowledge, however, that he does supply a valid basis for a deeper understanding of the question, in that he makes the distinction between what is present in the Eucharist by virtue of the sacrament or the words, and what is there by virtue of natural concomitance. In reality, therefore not only is the flesh and blood of Christ really present under the sacramental species and in each of their parts, but also his soul and divinity.

Actually the divinity was never separated either from the body, the blood or the soul of Christ; the soul that was separated from the body and the blood during the three days of his death, since body and blood were then separated, after the resurrection is really and forever united with them as the body is to the blood.

"If various things are really conjoined, where one of these really is, there also is the rest. What is really united can be looked at separately only through a logical process."[58]

However, logically speaking, when we begin with the direct meaning of the words that confect the sacrament, the body, blood, soul and divinity which are really present in either species and in each part, are present in accordance with a certain logical precedence. The words point directly to the body under the species of bread and the blood under the species of wine. Therefore, through the words, in which the sacrament is confected, we shall say that the body alone is present under the species of bread and the blood alone under the species of wine.

---

57. **Ibid.**
58. **Summa** III 76 a 1 c.

If under the species of bread there is also the blood and under the species of wine also the body, and under both species both soul and divinity are present, this is not because of the words, but because of the natural concomitance through which one of these things, in concrete reality after Christ's resurrection, is not present without the other.[59]

In this perspective we must then say that the Eucharist, logically speaking, from the viewpoint of the words and the signs that constitute the sacrament, is directly the sacrament of Christ's passion. In fact, the signs refer immediately not to the body in general nor to the blood in general, but to the body given or broken for men, and the blood shed for them: which points directly to the passion and the *Christum passum*.

However, since after Christ's resurrection the body, blood and soul are united by natural concomitance, the sacrament really contains the glorified Christ (a different Christ does not now exist) and unites us to him. Therefore, in this sacrament Christ who is present and from now on living and glorified, transforms us, or transforms us ever more intensely into his living and glorious self. Thus the Eucharist is also in a very real way the Easter of resurrection.

It does not unite us to the dead Christ, but to the Christ who had suffered (*Christum passum*) and who is now living and glorious forever.

c) The Eucharist as the end and the perfection of all the sacraments

Not the least among St. Thomas' merits is that he deduced with remarkable clarity the consequences that the doctrine of the Eucharist, seen in the context of the importance of Christ's body and ours in the economy of salvation, implies in regard to the unity of the sacramental complex (as well as that of

---

59. **Ibid.**, and ad 1 and ad 2.

the whole life of the Church) centered about this sacrament, and in regard to its necessity for obtaining salvation.

On the first point, St. Thomas was influenced by two statements of the pseudo-Dionysius in the third chapter of *De Ecclesiastica Hierarchia*. The first statement was that the Eucharist is *teleute teleutôn,* which we might translate as "initiation of initiations," or "perfection, end, consummation of initiations," and again "perfection, consummation, end of the sacraments." In his second statement, Dionysius observes, in reference to the Greek liturgical usage, that in the administration of all the other sacraments the apex and consummation of the rite is the Eucharist.

St. Thomas makes equal use of both texts and translates the first in various ways. He therefore says that the Eucharist is:

1) The perfection of perfections. The highest perfection of every thing consists in its being conjoined to the supreme principal from which it has its being. The Eucharist is conjoined with Christ, body, soul and divinity, who is the supreme principal and mediator of the being of the Christian life.[60]

2) The Eucharist is furthermore the perfection of the other sacraments, because it is conjoined not only with the salvific power of Christ, as are the other sacraments, but to Christ himself who is the source of that power.[61] It is so also because we can ascribe to the Eucharist the effects of all the sacraments since it contains, in a concentrated and resumptive way, everything that each one considered singly possesses.[62]

3) The Eucharist is the end toward which the other sacraments are directed; they mesh together in a preparatory function leading to it. St. Thomas takes support here from liturgical usage, following Dionysius, with an analysis of each individual sacrament.[63]

---

60. 4 d 8 q 1 a 1 q 1 c.
61. **Summa** III 75 a 1 c.
62. 4 d 8 q 1 a 2 q 2 ad 4.
63. **Summa** III 65 a 3 c. See also 63 a 6c.

Their order is directed toward the fulfillment of the Eucharist: the goal of baptism is to make man capable of receiving the Eucharist, and confirmation as the completion of baptism acts similarly, according to St. Thomas: "so that man may not draw back from it out of timidity." Penance and its complement, the anointing of the sick, have as their goal to purify man of sin committed after baptism in order that he might approach the Eucharist; marriage, "at least by its meaning refers to the union between Christ and the Church and is symbolized by the Eucharist."

If in the order of execution and practice, baptism comes first, as a preparation for the Eucharist, the Eucharist comes before baptism in the order of intention.[64] Therefore there is no denying that from the viewpoint of a systematized theology we must follow an ontological order which specifies that our first consideration be directed to what is determining, and only after that do we concern ourselves with what is determined by the former; therefore we should first treat of the Eucharist. If we commonly treat baptism first, this is merely because we are following the order of the sacraments as used by the faithful.[65]

In an incidental observation, St. Thomas states that the Eucharist is not only the end of all the other sacraments but also of all Church services: *finis omnium officiorum.*[66]

4) Thus the Eucharist in the Church is evidently the consummation of the other sacraments, which are directed toward it, while the Eucharist itself is not directed to any other sacrament:[67] "the term and the consummation of the spiritual life"[68] and man's sanctification. In brief, it is the apex of the whole

---

64. **Summa** III 73 a 5 ad 4.
65. 4 d 8 **Expositio Textus** at the beginning.
66. **Summa** III 65 a 3 ad 2.
67. **Summa** III 63 a 6 c.
68. **Summa** III 73 a 3 c.

life of the Church because "it joins the members to the Head"[69] and therefore "the entire mystery of our salvation"[70] is contained within it.

d) The necessity of the Eucharist for salvation

On the question of the necessity of receiving the Eucharist to obtain salvation, St. Thomas brings us an enlightening contribution by means of three distinctions.

The first is the distinction between the sacrament and the *res sacramenti,* more precisely for our purpose, between the pure sacrament and its spiritual fruit of salvation: Christ, incorporation in Christ, and the unity in the mystical body, charity and grace. The second is the distinction between the use of the sacrament *in re,* its effective use, and the desire or wish to receive it. The third is the distinction between the various ways of eating this sacrament.

a) a sacramental and non-spiritual eating of the sacrament: when the sacrament is received but without the requisite dispositions, the fruit of salvation is not received; b) a both sacramental and spiritual eating: when the sacrament is received and its fruits of salvation as well; c) a spiritual and non-sacramental eating: when without actually receiving the sacrament one still has the wish or the desire to do so and therefore receives the fruit of salvation from God.[71]

With this as a basis, here is St. Thomas' solution of the problem of the necessity of the use of the sacrament: man cannot attain salvation without the spiritual eating of the Eucharist which at least includes the desire actually to make use of it, and hence its use if the occasion presents itself: "spiritual eating includes the wish or the desire to receive this

---

69. 4 d 2 q 1 a 2 c.
70. Summa III 83 a 4 c. beginning.
71. Summa III 73 a 3 c. See also 68 a 3 c.; 80 a 1 a; a 2 c.; á 11 c.

sacrament, as we have said above (III, a 80, al, ad 3 and a 2 c.). Therefore without the wish to receive this sacrament man cannot have salvation. The wish itself, moreover, would be vain if it were not actuated when the occasion presented itself."[72]

There are throughout St. Thomas' work various important observations which further explain this basic solution of his.

We must especially point out that St. Thomas did not arrive at this solution from the very beginning. Here there is a marked evolution between the *Commentary on the Sentences*,[73] the commentary on St. John's Gospel[74] and the *Summa*.

His first solution was this: "the Eucharist *per se* is not necessary for salvation, but by the prescription of the Church, men . . . are obliged to receive it once a year."[75] In the second, however, he maintains that the Eucharist is necessary for salvation "not only by Church statute but by the Lord's command."[76] St. Thomas was at first unsuccessful in resolving the case of infants to whom in the Western Church the Eucharist was no longer administered. The solution to this difficulty he discovered later.

In the second place, we should point out that for St. Thomas: "the perfect way of receiving this sacrament is when one receives it in such a manner that at the same time he receives its salutary effect,"[77] which is the perfect eating of the Eucharist, both spiritual and sacramental. Why is this? In a few texts, St. Thomas replies: because "actually receiving the sacrament produces its effect in a more plenary way than its mere reception by desire."[78]

---

72. **Summa** III 80 a 11.
73. 4 d 9 a 1 q 2; d 13 q 3 a 2 q 1.
74. **In Jo. cap. VI, lect.** 7.
75. 4 d 9 a 1 q 2.
76. **Summa** III 80 a 1c.
77. **Summa** III 80 a 1c.
78. **Summa** III 80 a 1 ad 3; cf. III 69 a 4 ad 2.

The solution seeks to give an answer to a real problem. If through the mere desire or wish for the sacrament, God grants its fruit of salvation, it might seem that it is enough to have the desire without ever taking the care actually to receive it. But this would be to foster the way for eucharistic spiritualism that is asacramental and aliturgical. A danger that is not chimeric!

We may doubt, however, that this solution resolves the problem. But we must agree, I think, that in the perspective that seems to be that of article 11, question 80, the need to receive the Eucharist when one has the opportunity comes from another fact. If God grants the spiritual fruit of the sacrament even to the mere desire of receiving it on the part of one who does not have the opportunity of actually receiving it, he still never grants it without relation to the sacrament and its actual reception. It is quite natural that a person having the desire for the sacrament receive it when he has the opportunity: otherwise his desire would not have been true or sincere.

What is important here is to stress that men do not have grace from God without relation to the sacrament of the Eucharist. And this is precisely on account of the great general law of God, freely but wisely observed in the economy of salvation: *caro salutis est cardo.* To be united with Christ merely in a spiritual way, by charity and contemplation, without relation to the sacrament of the Eucharist, is not the human way of salvation, according to St. Thomas. Yet it is the way in which the angels are united with Christ, a purely spiritual way without any reference to the sacraments.[79]

It is still no less important to have brought into relief the fact that the lack of opportunity of receiving the sacrament is not an impediment to obtaining from God its spiritual fruits when the wish or desire for receiving it is present. Why is that? On this point, St. Thomas sends us back to what he had

---

79. 4 d 9 a 2 q 4 and 5. **Summa** III 80 a 2.

said about the efficaciousness of baptism of desire:[80] "the desire for baptism proceeds from faith working through charity; in virtue of this faith God, whose power is not bound to the visible sacraments, sanctifies the man inwardly,"[81] seeing men's hearts as he does.[82] Thus we find ourselves back with the other great law: that salvation is granted not to the bare sacraments nor to mere faith and charity, but to faith-charity and the sacraments, to faith-charity embodied in the sacraments. It is a unique way of salvation that has a twofold aspect to it: the faith-charity is determinent with regard to the outward ritual. It is the primacy of faith-charity over the external rite, although this faith-charity is not authentic unless also related to the external rite.

From the doctrine of the necessity of the sacraments, at least *in voto*, we are able to understand also the true import of the principle that God has not bound his power to the sacraments. He has not bound it to the actual use of the sacraments, but freely bound it to the sincere desire for the sacraments which also involves their actual use when the opportunity presents itself.

What kind of desire for the Eucharist and the sacrament in general does St. Thomas require in order to obtain grace? The examples he gives are always of an explicit desire. He did not yet discover the notion of implicit desire that was to be developed by later theology. Yet this has no small importance for an understanding of the whole extension of the necessity of the sacraments and especially the Eucharist for salvation, and the real force of the axiom: *caro salutis est cardo.*

Still, in the *Summa,* in direct evolution from his previous works and within the perspective that theology had given him up to this point, St. Thomas resolves the question of infants

---

80. **Summa** III 73 a 3 c.
81. **Summa** III 68 a 2 c.
82. **Ibid.,** ad 1.

which heretofore had embarrassed him. How are infants saved who have not received the Eucharist, if no one can attain salvation without at least the desire for the Eucharist?

Here he enlarges upon the solution given by St. Augustine to this difficulty: how can baptism be salutary for infants if baptism does not save without faith and infants cannot have faith? St. Augustine answers that infants believe by the faith of the Church.[83]

St. Thomas says: "through baptism, infants are directed towards the Eucharist. Therefore, by the very fact of their being baptized, they are directed by the Church to the Eucharist. Thus in the same manner that they believe through the faith of the Church, they desire the Eucharist through the Church's intention and consequently receive its *res*, its fruit."[84]

Hence St. Thomas can state this general principal: "no one has grace before receiving this sacrament or before having the desire to receive it, a desire made on his own by an adult, and for infants the desire of the Church."[85]

Yet it does not follow from all that has been said that communion *must* be always distributed under both species, since the whole Christ is contained even under one species.[86]

---

83. **De pecc. meritis et remiss.** I 25 PL 44, 131; I 19 PL 44, 123; and other texts cited by St. Thomas, **Summa** III 68 a 9 ad 1.

84. **Summa** III 73 a 3 c.

85. **Summa** 79 a 1 ad 1.

86. **Summa** III 80 a 12.

VII
CONCLUSIONS:

TOWARDS A BETTER UNDERSTANDING OF THE BASES OF THE LITURGY IN THE LIGHT OF THE AXIOM: *CARO SALUTIS EST CARDO*

This lengthy investigation which we have just completed has a threefold purpose: 1) to demonstrate that the doctrine of the "flesh as the pivotal point of salvation" which is so little known today in theology, spirituality and pastoral theology, has deep-seated scriptural, patristic and theological roots; 2) to make people aware of the fact that it is of enormous breadth and depth, and that it is of inestimable value as a synthetic general principal in enabling us to understand and give order to a vast area of data relative to the economy of salvation; and 3) to draw people's attention to the necessity of considering the liturgy in the light of this principle. For it is only in this way that we can have a better understanding of some of the liturgy's more central aspects, which, despite their singular theological, spiritual and pastoral weight, have only to some extent managed today to penetrate the consciousness of many theologians and pastors. This has happened, I think, because their minds have been formed in an anthropological climate that is quite different from that in which the liturgy is immersed and which our aphorism *caro salutis est cardo* supposes and expresses.

Let us now bring together the threads of our inquiry in order to show the essential theoretical structure of the views disclosed by this axiom. We shall prescind from reviewing the exegetical and traditional documentation which we have already discussed sufficiently in the preceding pages.

1) *Anthropology and liturgy in general*

At the very beginning, we must understand that anthropology (a particular way of understanding man in general, his nature, his destiny, his *modus agendi*) is one of the indispensable bases of christology.

In addition to the doctrine of the Church, which we have not considered in this study, it is also at the basis of the theology of the sacraments, and chiefly of the Eucharist; this is the pivotal point of the liturgy which is wholly built around the sacraments. Anthropology is thus a determining factor in christology, sacramentology and the liturgy.

This might seem strange but it is not in fact. In communicating with his creatures, God respects their nature and their natural way of acting. If this were not true, we should be faced with a contradiction since he himself is their author. If at times he may act above and beyond their natures, he never acts contrary to them.

This might seem strange but it is not in fact. In communicating with his creatures, God respects their nature and their natural way of acting. If this were not true, we should be faced with a contradiction since he himself is their author. If at times he may act above and beyond their natures, he never acts contrary to them.

Thus, if we have a poor understanding of man and his way of behaving, we shut ourselves off from an understanding of God's way of acting towards men, and the way in which he requires man to act towards him. This means that we would find ourselves cut off from the means of understanding the economy of salvation willed by God: from the incarnation through christology, soteriology, ecclesiology, the sacraments, moral, asceticism and mysticism. Obviously this also includes the liturgy.

It is urgent today that liturgical theology probe much more deeply into all the ramifications of the relations between anthropology and the liturgy.

If we have followed this analysis, we shall understand why it is permissible to regret that in the definitive text of the first chapter of the Constitution on the liturgy of Vatican II, contrary to what was present in the original composition, which served as its basis, there is no allusion to their anthropological foundation in the manner of presenting the incarnation and the nature of the liturgy, no allusion to human nature as being composed of body and soul.

This happened since there seemed to be no attempt at basing it on philosophical notions, which will certainly seem strange to anyone who knows how much Scripture and both patristic and theological tradition presuppose this general anthropological basis or even refer explicitly to it (for Scripture, see Hebrews 2:10-18, for example) in expressing the doctrine of the flesh as the pivotal point of salvation.

2) *Man's corporeity, the law of the incarnation and the law of sacramentality*

Man not only has a body but *is* a body, vivified by a spiritual soul which is precisely what makes him a *human* body.

The body receives the soul's influx and is conditioned by it. But at the same time, in another order of causality, it also influences the soul and conditions it. There is a reciprocal interdependence.

Man's welfare is not the welfare of the soul alone, but of

the composite unity of body and soul. The body is therefore the soul's instrument but not merely to attain its own welfare but rather the welfare of the whole. The soul cannot attain its very own "good," without also attaining the "good" of the body at the same time.

The body is the one means of communication between men and hence the basis of every human society. There is nothing of directly communal social value among men unless it agrees to pass through the body.

Only through his body does man communicate and unite with the sub-human world. Although not solely, man's body is the kernel of cosmic unity, because only there is matter in substantial union with spirit. For this reason, man is a *microcosmos*.

All obvious things are truisms, but they are nonetheless true and their consequences have not been sufficiently thought through.

a) In general

If the divine life was given to man, with respect for his nature and connatural way of acting, it must also in its own way have been given to the body; the body through the soul, but in other respects, the soul through the body. Therefore if it is true that the soul conditions the body, it is also true that the body, in other areas, conditions the soul.

This means that if God wishes to divinize man, respecting his manner of being and connatural mode of acting, this divinization can be nothing other than an "incarnation," a descent by God into man even in his flesh, and an elevation and assumption not only of the soul but also of the body of man in the divine life.

God cannot deter from observing this incarnational process once he freely decides to divinize man within the context of his modes of being and acting. In this precise sense, the incarnation process is a law of the divine economy.

Similarly, if God decides to divinize man using modes that respect his own connatural mode of being and acting he must of necessity use those in which the divine and human converge, including the sensory, the corporeal. He must use means in which the communication of the divine comes about also through and in the sensory with a reciprocal conditioning toward the spiritual.

A connatural means for divinizing an incarnate being is itself incarnate. Through this means the divine is present in the human, including the senses, and operates through the human, including the sensory, in order to raise man even in the sphere of the senses to a divine level of being and acting.

These means in the most general sense are called sacraments: human and sensory means that as instruments of the divine power contain this divine reality and communicate it to those who are well-disposed.

Hence this communication of divine life through the sacraments, defined in this way, is a law in the relations between God and man. God cannot deter from observing it once he decides freely to use means that are connatural to man's modes of being and acting, in the divinization of man.

The law of sacramentality is a particular instance of the more general law of the incarnation.

The laws of the incarnation and sacramentality in the means used will be all the more valid the more that God in the divinization process of man treats him in accordance with the exigencies of his social nature; in such a way that individuals within this same process become conjoined with one another and interact. In fact, it is through sensory things and the body that men's social communications take place. Hence, if the communication of divine life is to be made with respect to man's social nature, it can only be made in an incarnate and sacramental manner.

And since man in his body is bound to sub-human creation, to the entire material cosmos that surrounds him and which he links in himself with the higher world of the spirit, man's divinization in reference to his body in some way involves the whole cosmos which through man's body becomes man's theater and framework. The descent of the divine into the body of man implies and in a certain way *is* the transfiguration of the entire cosmos.

If this cosmic unity, which has its focal point in the human body, comes to be conceived, as modern sciences rightly suggest, not as something merely static, but as a dynamic thing, then man's divinization, on account of the focal position occupied by his body between matter and spirit, takes on the significance of a triumphal resolution, by divine condescendence, of a cosmic drama that has involved the whole physical, biological and zoological history of the world from the very beginning. In fact, this same human body, which God in his condescension to man has assumed into the cycle of the divine life to the extent his nature can tolerate, here appears as the result of a labor of tension which under the Creator's direction pervades the whole of material creation into the very vitals of its being.

In this light, lesser creation through the activity of perhaps millions and millions of years and the convergence of an infinity of secondary causes, and through the production of ever more perfect organisms tends toward the formation of a most perfect organism at its summit. In making this organism into a human body through the infusion of a human soul, with perhaps minimal morphological changes, and in uniting this human body to himself in the divine life in the manner and with the sacramental means we have mentioned, God has fulfilled the most profound meaning of this labor and of the history of the cosmos. Out of plurality and scatteredness, he has brought unity while safeguarding the necessary distinctness of his creation.

Here we have regained the sense of the harmony and the static and dynamic unity of the universe and the various orders of being from the lowest to the most exalted. We see reaffirmed the great intuition of neo-Platonism, Irenaeus and Teilhard in its most valid points, on the basis of Scripture and a tradition that is more authentic and more lived in a special way every day in the liturgy!

We now can witness the full cosmic value of the laws of the incarnation and sacramentality as derived from the corporeity of man.

For our purposes, we shall leave aside the moot question of whether the Word would have become flesh had man not sinned. These laws of the incarnation and sacramentality, for the reason we have mentioned, do not depend upon the hypothesis of man's sin or weakness contracted as a consequence of sin. They depend merely from the structure of human nature and the cosmic unity that pervades all things and is climaxed in the human body.

b) In Adam

And it is for this reason that these laws are applied together in man even before sin. In Adam divinization was, in its way, given to his body, and had he not sinned, it would have finally penetrated him totally. This is the meaning of the preternatural gifts, especially that of immortality.

As for the sacramental system before sin and in the case that man had not sinned, we ought in my opinion to subscribe to what Scheeben has to say against the negative solution St. Thomas posed to the problem. Aquinas, on this precise point, has preserved a curious trace of the disincarnate spiritualism of the Platonists and Neo-Platonists in the way he looked upon human nature in the state of innocence and the *raison d'être* of the sacramental system which is too limited to a merely medicinal function against the weaknesses of sin. The sacramental system in the state of innocence is denied, because, says St. Thomas, in man in this state everything was upright; therefore in him "his superior part dominated the inferior, *and was in no way dependent upon it. . . .* It would have been contrary to this state, if the soul in the same state were dependent for its attainment of perfection, whether of knowledge or grace, upon something material that is done by the sacraments; and therefore in the state of innocence, man had no need of sacraments, not only because these are aimed at a remedy for sin, but also since they are directed towards the perfection of the soul."[1] We might well wonder in this case what there was for the body to do in this state of innocence and what its usefulness for the welfare of the whole composite was. This mode of expression, it seems to me, is also contrary to so many of the observations St. Thomas makes about man in general and the state of innocence specifically. They have quite a different ring about them.

In any case, this is Scheeben's observation: "We are not at all inclined to deny that the supernatural institutions of Christianity have a medicinal function, an efficacy for the healing of human infirmity. We do not deny that the Son of God has come down to us in human nature, and still continues to dwell among us with His substance and power under a visible, sensible veil, in order to assist us in our weakness. Nor do we deny that our feeble powers are able to form a vivid notion of the supernatural, or even the spiritual, only under some sensible guise. Nevertheless we believe that something much deeper lies at the bottom of the whole sacramental order.

"Our stand is based on the doctrine we have laid down about the mystery of the first man in his original state, and the mystery of the God-man. Already in Adam we observe a distinctive and remarkable interlacing of supernatural grace with the nature of man, even with his material side. The transmission of grace in that state was bound up with the transmission of nature. But since the generative faculty of human nature depends on the material component of that nature, and is exercised by a material act that is perceptible to the senses, grace also was bound up with the same act; grace was to come to

---

1. Summa III 61 a 2.

Adam's descendants through the placing of this act, and hence in a sacramental manner, although in a fashion different from what is the case with the Christian sacraments.

"The reason for this sacramental connection was evidently not to impress upon Adam's descendants, by means of a sensible act, an awareness of the grace imparted to them; at any rate this aspect is secondary. The reason must evidently be sought in the fact that God wished to treat grace as a good of the race as such, to link his supernatural fruitfulness with man's natural fruitfulness, to join both together in one harmonious whole, and thereby to give to the former a natural substratum and to the latter a supernatural consecration. Just as the material side of human nature was to have part in the supernatural transfiguration blossoming forth from grace, and grace was one day to manifest its splendor even in man's corporal nature, so, too, man's corporal nature was meant to become the vehicle for the grace in which the whole human family was to share. This is a truly imposing arrangement, from which we learn how wonderfully the divine wisdom intended to join the highest to the lowest, so that both would represent the fullest harmony of the universe in mysterious unity and mutual dependence, and so that what was high would display its mighty energy in what was low, and the low in turn would be raised from its native lowliness to share in the power of the high. Such was the sacramental character of the first man's original state, and such its sublime meaning."[2]

It was worthwhile to quote this whole passage, since it would be hard to express this thought better. The incarnate and sacramental regimen of the relations between man and God in the last analysis is not based on a state of the decline of human nature, but simply on its essential corporeal structure and on the meaning this had in the constitution of human society and in cosmic unity.

---

2. The Mysteries of Christianity (St. Louis, 1946), pp. 563-584.

If we have not understood this properly, we shall always tend to look upon the sacramental system in its broadest sense (and hence the liturgy also, which is its expression) as something from which the more spiritual a man is the more he should try to disentangle himself, in order to take refuge as much as possible in "pure spirituality" and personal interiority, considered as *the* ideal to be attained.[3]

3) *Christ's physical body as the basis of salvation and the centrality of the paschal mystery*

The fact of the incarnation of the Word with all that follows from it must be meditated upon in the light of all we have said. Once God decided that man's reparation was to be made by the Son, and at the same time within the context of man's mode of being and acting as a spiritual, social and corporeal entity and in his body as the focal point of cosmic unity and a *microcosmos* in himself, it was obvious that everything came about through the incarnation of the Son of God and sacramentality.

Therefore "the Word became flesh . . . full of grace and truth . . . and of his fulness we have all received." Or, in St. Paul's words which are even more pregnant since they also mention sacrament, faith and the cosmic value of the incarnation: "For in him the whole fulness of the deity dwells bodily, and you have come to fulness of life in him, who is the head of all rule and authority . . . and you were buried with him in baptism, in which[4] you were also raised with him through

---

3. This trend is manifested, for example, in J. and R. Maritain, **Liturgy and Contemplation** (New York, 1959). See my article on this point: "**Contemplazione nella liturgia e Contemplazione fuori della liturgia**" in **Rivista di ascetica e mistica**, 7 (1962), 8-34.

4. It seems certain to me that these words must be interpreted as referring to baptism, contrary to those who wish to refer them grammatically to Christ. To me this seems to be required by grammar, the sense of the sentence and St. Paul's teaching on baptism. The relative pronoun

faith in the working of God, who raised him from dead" (Colossians 2:9-12).

Here the great novelty is not the incarnation but the fact that the very person of the Word became incarnate. A body is assumed not only into the sphere of divine life, but is made the body of the Word. Through him a human nature, including the body, becomes not only the Head of men but also the Head of the angels. And this nature seems to be, and in the mind of God to have been from the beginning the center and the firm basis of the whole human, sub-human and angelic universe, and the focal point of their convergence (Colossians 1:15; Ephesians 1:10; 1:20-23; Philippians 2:5-11; Hebrews 1:2-4).

Chalcedon's formula merely strengthens and specifies these perspectives: the union of human nature, including the body, in the person of the Word is without confusion and inseparable,[5] and, for completeness, we should add: for the safeguard of that hierarchy whereby human nature was and is the living and conjoined instrument of the divine person, and subject to him.

Moreover, the novelty is not sacramentality in act, but the sacramentality through which men by rite and faith are placed in contact with this same Son of God incarnate, with what he did and suffered in his flesh, and hence by means of his body they are assimilated to him and made sharers in his divine life.

Therefore, the physical body of the Son of God incarnate is and shall remain forever in eternity the instrument of divinity, the source and pivotal point of every divine communication and consequently of cosmic unity as well. It is in relation-

---

ho is too distant from the noun Christ; and it makes no sense to translate the passage: "in which Christ, you are also raised with him," while it does make sense to say: "by which baptism you were also raised with him," as a corollary to having been buried with him in baptism. See also Romans 6:3-12.

5. See **Conciliorum oecumenicorum decreta** (Herder, 1962), pp. 31ff, 62.

ship to this and to all that happens in it that the faith and the sacraments take on their full salvific value.

To this extent, then, the divine life and its transmission to creatures is linked up with things that are also material and acts that also involve the senses: especially with those sensory acts that Jesus performed and suffered in his flesh from the first moment of the incarnation to his sitting at the right hand of the Father.

Therefore, the Word operated through all that Christ did and suffered in his flesh. He is present in all places and at all times. Through all that Christ did and suffered in his flesh the divine life was and is communicated to men.

It was and is communicated as through an instrumental cause, and through an exemplary cause as well. In fact, in every grace that an individual receives, a human nature, as exemplified and participated in what took place in Christ, is assumed or ever more intensely assumed by God. It is born or born ever more intensely to a new life; dies or dies all the more to sin; rises or rises all the more to a new life in God. It has the right and the hope as long as it preserves this life, to ascend one day into heaven and there to reign with Christ at the right hand of the Father.

Finally, all that Christ did and suffered in his flesh from the first moment of the incarnation to his last breath on the cross, influenced and does still influence every grace given to men as a meritorious cause.

Thus man is always and must always be under the influence of the divinely vivified and lifegiving flesh of Christ, and of all that he did and suffered in his flesh as the instrument of the Word.

The culminating and resumptive point of all that Christ, from the incarnation to the ascension, did and suffered in his flesh is the passion, death and resurrection of the Word incarnate: his paschal mystery.

Why is this? All that he did from the first moment of the

incarnation to the last breath on the cross was meritorious and sufficient for the salvation of the world. But on the historical plane willed by God and accepted by Christ the meritorious works of the incarnate Word in the redemption had to include his passion and death. Without this the redemption would not have taken place. Therefore the other works on the historical plane would in fact have had no meritorious redemptive value except insofar as they were united with the passion and death. As all the rest the passion and death themselves were not what God desired and in fact what redeemed us except insofar as they were the culmination of Christ's whole redemptive life.

The life of the incarnate Word is *one,* one unique life's breath. The fullness of merit is attained only with the last breath upon the cross.

Yet, our divinely willed salvation was not merely that pardon for sins and grace were merited for us by the incarnate Word. It also included the notion that this same grace be continually applied to us by that same incarnate Word, now risen from the dead and in glory with the Father. Why so? Because as long as the incarnate Word remained in a humiliated, non-glorious state, and even more in a state of death — all consequences of sin, to which he agreed to submit in order as our Head to profess his obedience to God in ransom for our own disobedience — sin was not totally overthrown in his own flesh.

The plenary application of salvation through Christ's flesh therefore necessarily involved his prior plenary victory over death in his own flesh, which is the resurrection.

Thus Jesus' whole life, whatever he did or suffered in the flesh, has for its ideal focal point (which permeates everything and gives to everything that value that God willed it to have) the resurrection to the glorious life through his experiencing the passion and death.

This means that everything in Jesus is centered upon the paschal mystery. Or better, the mystery of Jesus is the paschal mystery. Hence it is not simply the mystery of the incarnate

Word but the mystery of the Word incarnate in the form of a servant who through his passion and death passes into the life of glory.

It is in this whole dynamic trajectory that Christ's physical body — what he did and suffered in his flesh — is the focal point of our salvation.

4) *Our saving contact with Christ's flesh, with what he did and suffered in his flesh, through faith and the sacraments*

In Christ, as Head of mankind, the fullness of divinity dwells bodily, because he communicates it to us and makes us sharers in it.

By right, every single human individual is divinized in this same incarnation, dies to sin with Christ in his death and rises with him in his resurrection, in the sense that each human individual can and must participate in these realities manifested in Christ's human nature, as the first fruits which by right are to be followed by many similar fruit.

Since these realities are given also to Christ's body and every human body is called to be a recipient of them, we must say — granted that the whole of creation finds its pivotal point and its unity in man's body — that in what happened in Christ's body, the entire cosmos is concerned and in its own way involved in the glorious transformation. Christ's body is the first fruits not only of men but of all creation.

And all of this is by right. Yet how will what Christ did and suffered in his flesh be communicated *de facto* to each man?

We know that since man's connatural way of being divinized is by means of the incarnation, his connatural means of receiving and transmitting the divine life in an incarnate way are means of a sacramental type. Saving contact with the flesh of Christ and with what he did and suffered in his flesh will therefore be of a sacramental kind connaturally.

This will be a contact that will join us to the whole Christ, divinity and humanity, soul and body, but beginning with the body, and it will involve our soul and our body, but, again, beginning with the body.

Scripture, tradition and theology speak of faith — a faith shaped in charity — and sacraments.

These are not two paths, but one unique incarnate path.

Faith-charity and the external rite concur to form together the saving sacrament, the sacrament that actually vivifies the recipient because it puts him in saving contact with Christ's body and with what he did and suffered in the flesh.

Faith-charity alone, without reference to the external rite, does not save.

Therefore such a faith does not really exist since the faith that saves is necessarily faith in the incarnate Word who suffered, died and rose from the dead, and now transmits the divine life to believers by means of the rites established by him.

To exclude from faith the efficaciousness of the sacraments as instruments whereby the Word Incarnate transmits life to believers, means that we do not have the faith that saves. This always includes the sacraments.

The same is true in its own way for charity: we do not love God unless we give heartfelt consent to the rites established by him for obtaining life.

Similarly, the external rite alone without faith-charity does not save. Both save together.

However, although faith-charity is not sustaining without reference to the rite, it does have primacy over it. When it is impossible for us to make outward use of the rite of the sacraments, absolutely or hypothetically necessary for salvation, God grants the salutary fruit of the sacrament to the desire or wish itself, precisely in virtue of the faith and charity that such a desire implies.

As in the incarnate Word himself, and in man in general, in the salutary sacrament there is a concurrence of faith and rite, spirit and matter, without confusion and inseparably, but under the primacy of the spirit, of faith-charity, over the bare external rite.

Still we must point out that faith does not end with the bare rite, but with the object signified by the rite as a sign: Christ himself and what he did and suffered in his flesh.

Therefore faith is superior to the bare sensible sign but not to the object it signifies. Faith is given its norm by the object signified by the sign.

Consequently, in the sacramental system there is a concurrence of a subjective element, faith; an external sensory element, the sign; and the object signified by the sensible sign, Christ. Faith is given its norm by Christ, but through the objective mediation of the sensible sign of the sacrament actually received, or at least received by desire. This is precisely the special characteristic of the sacramental way and of the dependence of the spirit on the body. However this does not go so far as to say that faith can never be united with Christ and receive his life-giving influence without the actual use of the sensory rite. Where there is an impossibility one's sincere desire is enough.

It is necessary to add with later theology, which on this point has rightly perfected the position of the Fathers and the Schoolmen, that when the actual use of the rite is impossible, the wish or desire to receive it can be not only explicit, as in one who knows the sacraments and wishes to receive them, but also implicit, since an implicit faith exists. This happens in a person who through no fault of his own does not know Christ and the true Church but still lives, informed by a remainder of grace, in accordance with the right dictates of his conscience, and is disposed to do all that God desires of him once he knows what that is. Such a person has an implicit faith in Christ and in the Church, an implicit desire to enter the Church and to use her sacraments. God gives him grace precisely on account of his implicit faith and his implicit desire for Christ, the Church and the sacraments.

It is important to note here that even a man of this kind is saved through salutary contact with Christ's flesh and with what he did and suffered in the flesh, through faith and the sacraments of the faith which he implicitly desires.

All of this is valid not only for men who lived after Christ, but also for those who, after the sin of Adam, lived before him. Since they were not saved without at least an implicit faith in Christ, neither were they saved without at least an implicit desire for the Church and the sacraments. For those who lived under the Mosaic law matters were even more specified by the prefigurative value of the sacramental rites of the Old Law in relationship to Christian sacraments, specifically the figurative value of circumcision in relation to baptism, and of the paschal lamb in regard to the eucharistic mystery.

In every case, the desire for the sacrament is sincere only in a person who, once he has some awareness of the necessity of the sacraments and is able to avail himself of them, also makes actual use of them.

From this we can see that the axiom "God has not bound his grace to the sacraments" is understood in the sense that he did not necessarily bind it to the actual use of the sacramental rite, although he truly and also voluntarily bound it at least to the implicit desire to use them.

This is the typically Christian balance between flesh and spirit, interiority and exteriority, subject and object.

Faith without reference to rite leads to subjectivism and ultimately to naturalism. Rite without faith leads to exteriorism, superstition and magic. Faith and rite inseparably united, under the primacy of faith over the bare rite and of the object of faith, Christ, over faith itself to which it gives the norm and which it qualifies, are this Catholic balance.

5) *The centrality of the eucharistic mystery seen in the light of the axiom*: caro salutis est cardo

The prospect opening before our eyes when we look at the economy of salvation in the light of the axiom *caro salutis est cardo* converges in the last analysis in the eucharistic mystery as the apex and source of this very economy.

a) It is the sacrament of the Body of Christ

If the flesh, and more precisely Christ's flesh is the focal point of all salvation and if man attains it only by means of the sacraments, the sacrament of the eucharistic mystery is the pivot, apex and source of all salvation because there and only there is the physical body of Christ really continued.

Naturally, on the condition that participation in the eucharistic mystery is salutary, that it takes place with a union of faith and charity and under the sensible sign of the species and the external rite, in the Eucharist we have the ideal contact, penetrating our soul and our body, with Christ's divinely vivified and life-giving flesh, and thereby with his soul and divinity, and consequently with the Son, the Spirit and the Father. "He abides in me and I in him." "We shall come into him and make our dwelling place in him."

b) It is the sacrament of the Christ's passion, death and resurrection and ours as well: the pre-eminent paschal sacrament

The pivotal point of salvation is not properly Christ's flesh considered statically, but his flesh acting and suffering for us and united sacramentally to us. In other words, it is what has happened and does happen in that flesh, actively or passively, in relation to our salvation and shared sacramentally by us. Moreover, as we have explained above, the center, culmination and source of what Christ did and suffered in his flesh is the passion and death, followed by the resurrection. It is also from this that the center, culmination and source of salvation is now the sacrament of the eucharistic mystery.

In fact, by virtue of the immediate meaning of the words and the signs in which it is accomplished, this sacrament directly refers to Christ's passion: the broken bread is Christ's body given for us, and the wine poured into the cup is Christ's blood shed for us. Now there is but one Christ. He once suffered and died, but is henceforth risen and glorious with the Father. He and no other is contained in the Eucharist. Therefore the sacrament of the Eucharist unites us to the body of Christ which suffered and died, but which passed through passion and death and is now risen and glorious with the Father forever.

Therefore, as the sacrament of the passion directly, the Eucharist is also the sacrament of the resurrection and the ascension, because of the natural concomitance of the body with the blood and the soul with both.

It is the sacrament of the entire paschal mystery of Christ himself, as the incarnate Word who suffered and died and is now risen and forever glorious with the Father.

Since this sacrament is given to us under the form of food in order to indicate the reciprocal identification that comes about in it between us and what the incarnate Word did and suffered in his own flesh (passion, death, resurrection and ascension), the eucharistic sacrament is not only the sacrament of the paschal mystery in Christ himself, but also of its extension in us. It is the pre-eminent Sacrament of the paschal mystery in the whole breadth of its extension: in Christ and in us.

Because of its likeness to and participation in what happened in the flesh of the Word incarnate who suffered and died to the power of sin and then rose to a divine life, and now reigns gloriously with the Father, it is above all in the participation in this sacrament that we also are in some way assumed by the divinity, die to sin and rise again to the divine life with the right and the hope of arriving at total and eternal glory with the Father.

It is true that this happens in some way in all of the sacraments, and chiefly in baptism which signifies directly the death and resurrection, and identifies us directly with the dying and rising Christ. The other sacraments do not do so directly but by means of the Eucharist, as we shall say further on, insofar as they imply at least a desire for the Eucharist. And this is because the other sacraments do not unite us to the very person of the dead and risen Christ, but only to a power derived from that person. The Eucharist alone, beginning with his flesh, unites directly to his own person.

Since the whole of Christian life is brought together in the participative extension to individuals of the mystery of the passion, death and resurrection of the incarnate Word, the eucharistic mystery, which in the light of *caro salutis est cardo* is the pre-eminent place in which this extension and participation takes place, is the center, apex and source of the economy of salvation.

c) It is the sacrament of the sacrifice of Christ and the Church

In what Jesus did and suffered and what he forever does and accomplishes in his flesh, and which has salvific value for us, there is a special place reserved for the worship which the incarnate Word, as our Head, offered and continues forever to offer to the Father. The supreme act of worship is sacrifice. Formally, this consists in a certain inward disposition whereby a man, in order to acknowledge God's total dominion, puts himself at God's complete disposal even to the heartfelt acceptance of the destruction of his own life if God so deems. If God does desire this destruction, the sacrifice will also be externally bloody, but the outward immolation will be a simple concretization of the inner disposition which alone gives sacrificial meaning to the act.

In Christ, this sacrificial disposition existed internally from the first moment of the incarnation and lasted throughout his life. Since, however, the Father also willed his actual bloody immolation and Christ accepted this from the first moment,

Christ's whole worship was focused on Golgotha and was actually accomplished only on Golgotha.

The sacrifice on Golgotha was externally and, as it were, materially, bloody and as such it ceased with the victim's resurrection. But in its spiritual and determinant aspect, Christ's interior disposition from which the whole salvific value of the external sacrifice was derived, remains unchanged and with his passover from time into eternity even eternal. The sacrifice of Golgotha in its spiritual and interior aspect, Christ's sacrificial disposition (and not in its bloody and material aspect), remains forever with the Father. It is Christ's heavenly sacrifice which continues the sacrifice of Golgotha in an unbloody way.

No one can be saved, if he does not participate in the worship, the sacrifice that Christ performed and performs in his flesh. And therefore the contact with what Christ did and suffered in his flesh comes about connaturally for us in a sacramental way. God also places us in contact with Christ's sacrifice by means of sacrament. The Mass is precisely the sacrament of the sacrifice of Christ.

The Church (and every man who participates in her with an identity of faith and charity, and in the external rite) makes this sacrifice of Christ her own, since she consents to the sacrifice that Christ as our Head makes of himself and of us, and she offers herself together with Christ to the Father. The Eucharist is the sacrament not only of Christ's sacrifice but also of the sacrifice of the Church.

If everything in the Church is directed toward the sanctification of man, this same sanctification of man is oriented toward the worship that man must give to God in Christ. At its summit, this sanctification is directed toward sacrifice as a participation in the sacrifice that Christ continues to perform (although in an unbloody way) in his flesh. This is to say that the whole economy of salvation is now centered on the Mass.

d) It is pre-eminently the sacrament in which the Church is born, grows and subsists

The divine economy on earth has no other purpose but the birth, growth, subsistence and perfecting of the Church as the mystical body of Christ: the fellowship of those who are united to Christ Jesus, participate in his divine life, and thereby are united with God and with one another.

But since the flesh of Christ is this pivotal point of every communication of divine life to men, and since this communication comes about by means of sacrament, in the last analysis, the Church is born, grows, subsists and perfects herself in reference to the physical body of Christ which she reaches and attains in the eucharistic mystery.

e) The culmination of the doctrine *caro salutis est cardo*

The logical consequences of all of this are clear as regards the place of the eucharistic mystery in the economy of salvation, in the light of the axiom *caro salutis est cardo*.

The other sacraments are oriented toward the eucharistic mystery, have the value of a preparation for it and confer grace only in virtue of a certain desire, which is at least implicit on the part of the one who receives them to participate in this eucharistic mystery. St. Thomas' doctrine on these points is the logical consequence of the doctrine of *caro salutis est cardo*: "no one has grace before receiving this sacrament or before having the wish to receive it";[6] baptism itself does not give grace, except in the case of infants, without a certain desire for the Eucharist;[7] only the Eucharist gives grace by its own

---

6. Summa III 79 a 1 ad1.
7. Summa III 73 a 3 c.

power, the other sacraments do so insofar as they share in it through the Eucharist.[8]

As for the necessity of participating in the eucharistic mystery in order to have grace, we must assert with the catechism of the Council of Trent, and in the strictest sense, that the Eucharist is "truly the source of all graces" for men on earth;[9] and without at least the implicit desire for the Eucharist "man cannot have salvation."[10]

All this merely re-echoes the peremptory statements in the Gospel of St. John which patristic tradition, and especially the Greeks, never forgot: "Unless you eat the flesh of the Son of man and drink his blood, you have no life in you; he who eats my flesh and drinks my blood has eternal life and I will raise him up on the last day. . . . He who eats my flesh and drinks my blood abides in me, and I in him. As the living Father sent me, and I live because of the Father, so he who eats me will live because of me" (6:53-57).

6) *The liturgy in the economy of salvation in the light of the axiom*: caro salutis est cardo

We can close this study with the simple statement . . . therefore the liturgy is the center, apex and source of the actual economy of salvation.

All that we have been saying has a directly liturgical value and helps us in understanding the liturgy: what we have pointed out about the law of the incarnation and of sacramentality, derived from the corporeity of man; what was said about the irreplacable function derived from it, within the

---

8. **De Veritate,** 27 a 4 c.

9. **Catechismus ex decreto concilli Tridentini ad parochos** (Rome, 1920), pp. 170-171.

10. St. Thomas, **Summa** III 80 a llc.

economy of salvation actually willed by God, for Christ's physical body, for what he did and suffered in his body culminating in his paschal mystery; all that has been explained about the essential function of the faith and the sacraments as a means of salutary contact of an incarnate kind with Christ's flesh and with what he did and suffered in that flesh; and finally the conclusions deduced from this with respect to the eucharistic mystery as a point in which the whole economy of salvation, focused upon Christ's flesh, is centered for us today. All of it shows the foundation for the liturgy's prerogative of being the privileged place of Christ's presence in the world, of the encounter of men with God in Christ Jesus. It is the culmination point towards which the whole life of the Church is directed, and the source from which its whole power springs; the junction of cosmic unity re-established in the flesh of the Lord.

This study had no other aim than to illustrate in a specific way articles 5, 6 and 7 of the Constitution on the Liturgy of the second Vatican Council, by linking its teaching, better than the Constitution itself does, to the general anthropological basis of man's corporeity, and interpreting it in the light of the axiom *caro salutis est cardo.*

It is sufficient to re-read the salient points of these articles in the light of what we have been saying in order to realize this.

"5. When the fullness of time had come (God) sent his Son, the Word made flesh, anointed by the Holy Spirit . . . to be 'a bodily and spiritual medicine,' the Mediator between God and man. For his humanity, united with the person of the Word, was the instrument of our salvation. Thus in Christ 'there came forth the perfect satisfaction needed for our reconciliation, and we received the means for giving worthy worship to God'. . .(Christ) achieved his task principally by the paschal mystery of his blessed passion, resurrection from the dead, and glorious ascension, whereby 'dying, he destroyed our death, and rising, he restored our life.' For it was from the side of

Christ as he slept the sleep of death upon the cross that there came forth the wondrous sacrament which is the whole Church.

"6. Just as Christ was sent by the Father, so also he sent the apostles, filled with the Holy Spirit . . . (that) they might proclaim . . . (and) exercise the work of salvation which they were proclaiming, by means of sacrifice and sacraments, around which the entire liturgical life revolves. Thus, by baptism, men are plunged into the paschal mystery of Christ; they die with him, are buried with him, and rise with him. . . . In like manner, as often as they eat the supper of the Lord they proclaim the death of the Lord until he comes. . . . From that time onward the Church has never failed to come together to celebrate the paschal mystery. . . .

"7. To accomplish so great a work, Christ is always present . . . in the sacrifice of the Mass . . . especially under the eucharistic species. By his power he is present in the sacraments . . . (because) the liturgy is considered as an exercise of the priestly office of Jesus Christ. . . ."[11]

These notions (which are the immediate framework in which the Constitution presents the nature and the prerogatives of the liturgy) take on, if I am not mistaken, a surprising new force in the light of our axiom: *caro salutis est cardo.*

The liturgy is nothing else than the celebration of the eucharistic mystery, encompassed by the other six sacraments which Christ willed to be preparatory to it, and framed within the celebration of the "little sacraments" or sacramentals instituted by the Church to emphasize to the fullest in the very style of the greater sacraments men's salutary contact with the life-giving flesh of Christ and with what he did and suffered in his flesh; in other words, with the unique source whereby they are permitted to attain salvation.

Therefore, the whole liturgy, including what was instituted

---

11. **Constitution on the liturgy** in **The Documents of Vatican II**, W. M. Abbott, S.J., ed. (New York, 1966), pp. 139-141.

by the Church, is built upon the axiom *caro salutis est cardo,*
and is incomprehensible outside of the concrete and biblical
anthropology that this axiom presupposes. Any tendency, even
an unconscious one, toward a dualistic notion of man, whether
it is of Gnostic type or influenced by the disincarnate spiritualism of the Platonists or Neo-Platonists, is fatal to the liturgy.
It is equally fatal to the statements: "The Word was made
flesh" and: "unless you eat the flesh of the Son of man and
drink his blood, you shall not have life in you." It is just as
deadly for an understanding of the real meaning of the paschal
mystery, its resumptive value in regard to the whole economy
of salvation and its strict connection with the eucharistic
mystery.

It is a dualism that ultimately excludes the possibility of a
full understanding of the force of the both static and dynamic
unity of the cosmos, which itself binds together (granting the
necessary distinctions) every order of being and has as its
focal point the body of man and more precisely, the body of
the God-Man.

All these notions stand out in brilliant relief in the Bible and
in the liturgy.